THE BRYANTVILLE METHODIST CHURCH
BOX 447
BRYANTVILLE, MASS.

Dynamics of Evangelism

Let
my Word
come
Alive

Dynamics of Evangelism

GERALD L. BORCHERT

Foreword by
LEIGHTON FORD

Word Books, Publisher
Waco, Texas

ISBN 0-87680-468-7

Library of Congress Catalog Card Number: 76-2866

Printed in the United States of America

To Dorie, Mark, and Timothy

Other books
by Gerald L. Borchert

GREAT THEMES FROM JOHN
THE DYNAMICS OF PAULINE EVANGELISM
TODAY'S MODEL CHURCH

CONTENTS

Foreword by Leighton Ford 9

Preface 11

Acknowledgments 13

1. The Outward Dimension 15

2. Ancient Clues for Modern Evangelists 23
   *An Evangelist's Lesson in the Struggle with Faith •
   An Evangelist's Lesson in Conquering Excuse • An
   Evangelist's Lesson in the Numbers Game • An Evange-
   list's Lesson in Insecurity • An Evangelist's Lesson in
   Painful Relationships • An Evangelist's Lesson in Re-
   jection • An Evangelist's Lesson in Hypocrisy*

3. Standards for Witnessing 45
   Revealing a Secret • Signs for Believing

4. Turning the World Upside Down 73

5. Advice for Struggling Evangelists 91
   *Encountering the Extraordinary Evangelist • Choosing
   the Evangelistic Model • Clarifying the Evangelistic
   Message • Developing an Authentic Evangelistic
   Community • Becoming an Effective Evangelist*

6. Future Perspective 121

7. Reaching Out 143

FOREWORD

The tides of evangelism are rising again throughout the world! Reports to the International Congress on World Evangelization at Lausanne, Switzerland, in July 1974 made that unarguably clear. More people are being reached with the gospel of Christ in more nations and in more ways now than ever before!

With this rising tide has come a flood of books and articles on evangelism. Many of these deal helpfully with the "how" of evangelism—methods, techniques, and programs. These are all vital; evangelism is nothing if it is not practiced. Equally urgent, however, is the confidence that our practice of evangelism is deeply rooted in Scripture. We must always ask of any approach two questions: Is it effective? Is it scriptural?

Gerald Borchert has done a great service by tying these two questions together in *Dynamics of Evangelism*. For several reasons, I am happy to commend this book to what I trust will be a wide readership.

First, it's always a delight, not to say a surprise, to meet a theologian and a seminary faculty member who has a passion for evangelism. James Denney, the Scottish divine, once remarked, "If evangelists were our theologians and theologians our evangelists, we would come nearer to the ideal church." This volume would please Denney. Gerald Borchert is an able theological educator who has a heart passion for evangelism. North American Baptist Seminary, where he serves in several capacities, has assigned to the work of evangelism a priority role in its life and ministry. They are committed to training students who have a burning passion to hold out the word of life to lost persons in a bewildered world. May their example infect all our professors and seminaries!

Again, I commend this book because it presents such a rich, strong biblical view of evangelism. Evangelism is not merely a part of the Bible; rather it is its very heart! Too often evangelists have been content to string together isolated verses of the Bible and call that a "theology of evangelism." Dr. Borchert shows that this approach misses the true force of the biblical teaching. Evangelism is the warp and woof of the whole of Scripture. From Genesis to Revelation it reveals God's great and eternal purpose of salvation. Evangelism is not to be found only in some texts from the Gospels and some stories from Acts. No! From the reluctant Moses of the Old Testament to the visionary John of the New, the would-be evangelist of the twentieth century can draw inspiration.

Finally, the author is not content to leave us with comforting theories. Throughout there is the challenging call to practical obedience. Biblical evangelism demands of us, not polite affirmations, but sacrificial involvement. Pastor, teacher, evangelist, lay witness—all who read will finally be left with the penetrating question of Jesus: "Why do you call me Lord, and do not the things I say?"

It is my prayer that *Dynamics of Evangelism*, with its fine combination of theological integrity, biblical truth, and practical passion, will lead many of us to a new obedience to the ever-contemporary mandate: "Go . . . and make disciples of all nations."

LEIGHTON FORD
Charlotte, North Carolina
July 1976

PREFACE

This book is intended for Christian lay people and ministers who genuinely desire to be more effective disciples of Jesus and who long to accept the Lord's summons on their lives for the task of evangelism. The Holy Bible is the Christian's evangelistic source book. It must be foundational to all discussion on evangelism. As a writer I make no apology for directing you to the Bible as you seek to discover the dynamics of evangelism. Indeed, I pray that this present study may be a tool to help you discover that evangelism is not simply an adjunct part of the Bible's message but is in fact related to the very essence of the organization and construction of the Bible and its theology. The Bible was written for the purpose of helping man discover the loving and searching God. My conscious goal has been to make that purpose clearer.

In finalizing this work, I am truly indebted to many people and experiences. To a number of friends who have read this manuscript and have made helpful comments; to my teachers from North America and Europe who in the past have encouraged me in academic investigation; to my students and colleagues at the North American Baptist Seminary who for more than a decade have asked me the difficult questions and have thereby forced me to integrate practice and theory; to the many professors, guides, and residents in the Mediterranean area who assisted me to greater reflection through relating the biblical texts to current geographical settings in all parts of the Middle East during the past few years and especially to those in Israel where I have lived and taught this year—to all these people who have made such

11

significant contributions to my life and work I express sincere gratitude.

Particularly, to my loving wife, Dorie, and my two sons, Mark and Timothy, who have endured the many absences through travel of their husband and father, I stand forever indebted.

Finally, to God who sent his son Jesus Christ, I as an admittedly weak follower of the Lord have gratefully come to realize that whether one is in the United States or the United Arab Republic, whether in Canada or the Cameroon, West Africa, God offers opportunities to witness for him. And even in some places where evangelism is regarded as illegal, Christ's servant who stands ready can be shocked to discover that in such circumstances God may offer authentic opportunities for genuinely relating the Lord Jesus to people who long to find the peace which comes from forgiveness and the joy which results from a proper relationship to God.

GERALD L. BORCHERT
American Institute of
Holy Land Studies
Jerusalem 1974

ACKNOWLEDGMENTS

Since returning to the United States and resuming my teaching responsibilities, I wish to express a special word of thanks to two friends. Leighton Ford, vice-president of the Billy Graham Association, has made me humbly grateful for his willingness to write the foreword to this book. Also I am sincerely indebted to Richard Gorsuch, a creative Christian commercial artist, who has supplied the graphic materials. Heavy Thinking is one of Rich's syndicated efforts to communicate the gospel in a contemporary art form through the local media. Since Rich is genuinely conscious of church budgets, I invite pastors and interested lay people to write him c/o North American Baptist Seminary, Sioux Falls, South Dakota 57105, for the privilege of using his materials in your area.

GERALD L. BORCHERT
Sioux Falls 1975

13

1
The Outward Dimension

what do you want most out of life?

THE OUTWARD DIMENSION

"I do not have the kind of personality that can buttonhole people and tell them they're going to hell."

"Don't ask me to be an evangelist. That stuff is O.K. for Billy Graham or Leighton Ford; God made them that way, but it's not my style."

"Why should I upset others and tell them they're lost?"

Anyone who has been involved in the work of evangelism has undoubtedly met many people with arguments, caricatures, and excuses. The problems people face in reaching out to others are not new and need to be understood by all Christians.

Recently a pastor said to me that he was desperately afraid to visit with people and speak to them about Christ. He felt comfortable behind the pulpit, and to his credit he preached rather well-constructed sermons having good evangelical content. But his fear of personally representing Jesus to people was so intense that he resigned his pastorate. Perhaps this minister was in the wrong vocation. Some would say that his psychological hang-ups or insecurities in the ministry were too much for him to bear. Such insecurity, however, is not an isolated experience but is felt by a significant number of Christian laymen and pastors. They seem to have low personal esteem and an intense fear of speaking about Jesus (although they have no trouble speaking about sports). Consequently, they often develop complex guilt feelings because of their failures to witness for Christ.

Some time ago while I was working with military chaplains, another encounter took place. A career army chaplain who had returned from Vietnam confessed to me that he could not stand being at the front when the wounded were brought in from the battlefield. He rejected the battlefield experience, not because of the sight of blood or because of any relationship to pacifistic orientations, but, as he put it, because he did not have anything from God to say to the soldiers. "O Lord," I thought, "nothing to say to a man who has lost half his body and is ready to die! What a tragic testimony of a chaplain's relationship to God." But then I stopped and asked myself, "What word do I have for dying people?"

On another occasion while flying between Lagos, Nigeria, and Cairo, Egypt, I was seated beside a well-dressed Egyptian physician. As I considered my relationship with this man, I found myself in a typical struggle of trying to decide whether or not I should say something of Christ to this Muslim. In standard fashion, my battle was not with the other man but with God and my own timidity. This time it was heightened by my concern to communicate with someone from a different culture. Yet, during the past month I had just been speaking to many African people of different cultures. Of course, I could make distinctions, but the battle with fear and excuse was with me once again. At this point I began to ask myself, "Why should I have such great difficulty speaking about the Christ I love so much?" And then I could not help but remember that as Christians we are not simply wrestling against flesh and blood but, as Paul indicates, we are in an outright war with the forces of evil. If we are to succeed in this conflict, we need the complete armor of God (Eph. 6:11–12). That full armament, including prayer (Eph. 6:18), was and continues to be my only hope for becoming one of Christ's human bridges over which the Lord Jesus can walk to others—whether they are from my own culture or from another.

In this witnessing battle with the devil, it is not a master's or doctor's diploma that enables one to respond to God's summons on one's life. Educational experiences, as Moses and Paul discovered, can be used by God, but effective response of a person to God's call on his or her life is quite different from meeting an educational requirement.

Indeed, in having been asked by a number of seminaries and other Christian institutions for interviews, never once have I been asked about my personal evangelistic interest and involvement. On several occasions I have had the opportunity to ask the faculties of some notable evangelical institutions why they did not ask me such a question, and I have been surprised by some red faces and saddened by some responses. Besides being a dean of a theological seminary, I teach New Testament—a field regarded as one of the most classical of seminary subjects. Now putting aside all friendly bantering that takes place among theological faculties throughout the country, I firmly believe that this outward dimension of the Christian life is absolutely crucial to the whole spirit of a seminary or a church. Like prayer and the devotional life, evangelism must never be taken for granted by Christian educators. Evangelism is at the heart of the Bible and must be so viewed in the life of all Christians.

While I am by no means suggesting that everything in the Holy Scriptures can be interpreted under the rubric of evangelism, I am suggesting that an interest in evangelism does not simply belong to the domain of practical theologians, pastors, and involved lay people. Is it not about time for sophisticated biblical scholars and theologians to recognize that we have written very little on this subject in decades? Unless we are invited to give a paper at some conference of the church, we probably give very little attention to this concern. I pray therefore, that we will not be too busy with textual criticism, *Formgeschichte,* existential philosophy, and so on to give a little time to supply the church with a better understanding of this aspect of its God-given ministry.

Moreover, a warning should be sounded to those who would bifurcate the message of Jesus and choose to emphasize either social concern or interest in personal redemption. Jesus both healed a paralytic and forgave the man's sins (Mark 2:1–12). Likewise, he taught people the way of life and fed their empty stomachs (Mark 6:34, 44). Whatever reasons Christians may give for neglecting either of these aspects of the gospel, let us not attribute to the Bible our incomplete representation of concern for others.

The story of the Bible is the wonderful account of the seeking God who loves the people of his creation and desires that they should come to know the blessing of an intimate relationship with their Creator. In this God-given Book, however, no attempt is made to hide the desperate situation of man with arguments or excuses. Throughout history God has acted repeatedly to lead men and women to acknowledge their sinfulness and to bring them to new life through faith. But, as the Bible says, in the fullness of time God effectively acted once for all in sending his only Son into the world (Gal. 4:4). That he was rejected and killed is the tragic testimony of the New Testament. That he was raised from the dead, however, is the startling news that has changed the course of history and has altered man's relationship with God. Communicating this exciting message and its meaning for the people of the world is the Christian's outward dimension—the work of evangelism.

Even though some believers have a special gift, nevertheless evangelism is the captivating task of *every Christian* in the church. For this task the Bible is and must be the Christian's source book. In the Bible is recorded the church's message of God's gracious wholeness for man and man's clear responsibility for his fellowman. To the Bible one looks for the goal and style of evangelism as one seeks to respond to God's summons on his or her life. From the Bible one receives genuine encouragement in the work of evangelism through the example of others who have been made alive by God's power and have literally shaken the structures of their society. Nevertheless, within the Bible one also encounters the striking reality of the suffering God and likewise discovers that Christian evangelists are not immune to persecution. Yet through the influence of the Bible and the witness of the Holy Spirit, the Christian evangelist is enabled to stand confident in the face of opposition knowing that, in the coming of Jesus Christ, the God of heaven and all creation is involved in this outward dimension of reaching others with the good news of life.

As you read the following pages, consider seriously the personal aspect of God's outward dimension for your life. Christians in many areas of the world are experiencing severe persecution. The era ahead may not be easy, but it is precisely at such times that Christians must be strengthened by God and reach out to others with the gospel in the name of Jesus. My personal prayer, therefore, is that some hesitant lay person, seminary student, or minister in reading here about evangelism may be helped to experience the thrill of a greater confidence in God and venture beyond the Christian community to witness to others about becoming alive in Christ.

2
Ancient Clues
for Modern Evangelists

FAITH

at the beginning is a fearful thing

ANCIENT CLUES FOR MODERN EVANGELISTS

The lives of the people of God in the Old Testament reveal perspectives which are often strangely similar to those of Christians involved in the task of evangelism. The stories in the Old Testament need not be simply tales from the past. They can live again and cry their messages to those of the twentieth century who know how to listen.

While many biblical stories have become so popular they have even been the subject of comic-strip presentations, a superficial reading of these stories can easily lead to a misconception of the biblical hero. The hero of the Old Testament is really not Abraham, Moses, Gideon, Elijah, Hosea, Jeremiah, Jonah, or any of the other well-known men or women. The hero of Scripture is God. The man or woman of God is a servant or instrument who is frequently rebellious, frustrated, and disillusioned. Moreover, he or she is generally placed as a spokesman for God within a social or community context in which he or she feels helpless. Yet despite human weakness, God uses his servant to bring both hope and judgment to people who are in need of understanding more fully the meaning of God's hand being present in this disjointed world.

The reactions of the Old Testament prophets and leaders can thus be very instructive for Christians who, despite acknowledged human weaknesses, are called by God to communicate the message of eternal life and its implications for a world on the threshold of "1984." [1] While many Old Testament personalities could have been selected for review in this chapter, a brief analysis of seven representative leaders is included. The fact that all are men in no way indicates a male chauvinistic view of evangelism. God knows the significant role women have played in the mission of the church. These particular men have been chosen because they seem to provide a helpful progression of thought. Moreover, the calls and the responses to God of these representatives show that the God who acted in the Old Testament age is the same God who acted decisively in Jesus Christ and who continues to act today by calling his people to the undiminished task of reconciliation.

An Evangelist's Lesson in the Struggle with Faith

Scarcely can one discuss God's call and the reactions of his servants in the Old Covenant without mentioning the patriach Abraham. The story of this man stands at a unique point in the Book of Genesis. The first eleven chapters, which have been the subject of great controversy among some scholars, can nevertheless be agreed by those of most theological traditions to form an important unit in the pattern of God's dealing with sinful mankind.[2] Each story, from the temptation by the serpent, through Cain's act of murder and the flood of Noah, up to the tower of Babel, ends with a statement of hope announcing God's continued attempt to restore and renew mankind. The episode of the tower of Babel, however, ends without such a redemptive note. The nations are scattered in hopeless disunification because of man's sin. Some answer to the plight of man is desperately needed. At this juncture the patriarch from Mesopotamia is introduced.

God called Abram to leave his country and his relatives and journey to a land which would be given to him (Gen. 12:1 ff.). This summons was not a purposeless, unreasoned act on God's part; it was designed to make an independent nation out of Abram's offspring. The nation, however, *was not to be an end in itself.* God intended that through this nation all the people of the earth would be blessed (12:3), a foundational theme for understanding evangelism. God's purpose is to save the entire world through the establishment of a community like Israel (or through a group of people like the Christian church).

But despite God's promise to Abram, the question remained, How could Abram become the father of a nation when he had no children? Yet Abram obeyed God's command. His little band packed their bags and left home. They traveled to Palestine, to Egypt, and back to Palestine. During this journey God reannounced his promise at Bethel (12:7) and in the Canaanite highlands (13:16). But Abram still had no children. Therefore, he urgently reminded God that his trusted servant Eliezer, the Syrian, would likely become his heir (15:2). God's reply was a strong reaffirmation of the promise through a dramatic covenant experience (15:5–21). But Abram still had no children! Then his wife suggested a substitute marriage arrangement with her servant woman similar to a custom discovered at ancient Nuzu. While this arrangement caused family frustrations, it was nevertheless fruitful. God, however, did not—and will not today—accept human ingenuity (like evangelistic gimmicks) as the answer to the fulfillment of his gracious promises. Instead, God again reaffirmed his covenant with Abram and gave the sign of circumcision.

Moreover, at ninety-nine years of age Abram was given a new name—Abraham, "father of a multitude." But in spite of a name change. Abraham still had no children. And who could not help but laugh with Abraham (17:15–21) and with Sarah (18:11–15) at the thought of a child being born to Sarah after the age of ninety when the menstrual flow had long since ceased? Yet Abraham accepted God's covenant and circumcised all the men and boys in his household as an acknowledgment of this acceptance. True to his word God gave Abraham and Sarah their long-awaited son, Isaac (21:1 ff.). God's promised miracle had come to pass at last.

But the trial of Abraham's faith concerning this son of the covenant was not yet completed. Genesis 22 recounts one of the most moving stories in the Old Testament, a story which establishes the reason Abraham is exemplified as the father of faith in the New Testament (see Rom. 4:16). In response to God's command to sacrifice his only son on Mt. Moriah, Abraham set out to follow the divine instructions. The deep pathos of this Hebrew story is reflected through the English translation in phrases like "your only son," "both of them went together," and "God will provide." All of Abraham's hopes are contained in this only son whom Abraham did not expect to bring back from Moriah. But despite the fact that his hopes would probably be destroyed, Abraham was willing to recognize God's authority above his own greatest desire. This recognition of the primacy of God is the mark of a faithful servant. In response, God substituted a ram and returned to Abraham *his only son*. Furthermore, God again reaffirmed his promised vow that Abraham's descendants would be greatly blessed and would be the means for blessing the world (Gen. 22:12–18).

To the contemporary Christian, the call of Abraham is exceedingly relevant. Not only does it provide an exemplary model of what it means for a human being to struggle with faith and wrestle with the call to be a servant of God in the context of real life, but it also provides an insight into the faithfulness of God with respect to his servants. To be an evangelist today necessitates a similar reliance upon God. Confidence in the faithfulness of God actually to work his will through his servant is a vital element in being an effective evangelist of the New Covenant. Without faith, the evangelist may as well capitulate to the atheistic, rationalis-

tic, naturalistic, self-centered authorities in the world. But
with faith in the power of God, the servant of God can challenge the world to reconciliation through the substitution-
ary death of Jesus Christ.

The story of Abraham is also extremely significant from
another point of view. It furnishes insight into God's perspective concerning the purpose for blessing Abraham and
his children. Among the people of God there is often a dead-
ening temptation which must be resisted with firm determi-
nation. This temptation is to forget that a concomitant
responsibility usually follows God's blessing. God's blessing
of Abraham's seed carried an easily overlooked announcement. The recipients of the blessing *were expected* to be a
blessing to the rest of the people of the world. In this way
God began to reverse the disunification of mankind represented at the tower of Babel.

Both in Israel and in Christianity, the blessings of God
have been accepted rather readily. The responsibility for
bringing the world to God, however, was not generally accepted by Israel and has been frequently avoided by Christians. What happened at first to William Carey (he was told
by his fellow Christians to sit down and let God save the
heathen) when in 1792 he sought to enlist support for a new
mission enterprise [3] has been repeated periodically in the
history of Christendom. To be a servant of God means that
one recognizes he does *not* deserve the blessing of God. Indeed, faith does not purchase God's blessing. But faith receives it and accepts the responsibility for sharing the
graciousness of God with the rest of God's creatures. Reaching out to others in evangelism, then, is not some optional
facet of Christian life. Sharing the blessings of the gospel is
implicit in accepting the call to be both a Christian and a
descendant of Abraham. To be a Christian clearly implies
being a witness.

An Evangelist's Lesson in Conquering Excuse

The student of the Bible cannot help but recall Moses'
novel rescue from the bulrushes by an Egyptian princess.
This occurrence undoubtedly provided Moses an opportunity
to prepare for God's call upon his life by supplying Moses
with the finest educational advantages and leadership experiences possible. Moreover, prior to his call, from the human point of view Moses' loyalty to his Hebrew heritage was
firmly established by his murdering an Egyptian taskmaster
who was whipping an enslaved Hebrew.

Yet at the burning bush, when God laid a commission upon
Moses, the reaction of this leader-designate was to emphasize
his human incompetence in comparison to Pharaoh's great
power. "Who am I," he answered, "that I should appear before Pharaoh and lead the children of Israel out of Egypt?"
(Exod. 3:11). God rejoined the discussion with precise instructions concerning the mission. Moses replied that no one
would believe God had personally appeared to him or given
him a task (4:1). God's retort was to provide two miraculous
signs which would forcefully indicate that Moses was representing God.

Unwilling yet to accept God's charge, Moses turned to a
clear excuse and virtually claimed that he was academically
and psychologically incompetent for the task (4:10). The
divine reply was that God was the creator of man's mouth.
Utterly frustrated with God's insistence, Moses cried in exas-
peration, "Send somebody else" (4:13). But Moses did not
gain his wish. God knew the nature of his servant's fear, and
when the supportive companionship of Aaron was provided,
Moses carried the message of God into the very den of the
Egyptian Pharaoh.

It seems to be a genuinely human phenomenon that God's
servants, like Moses, often feel a fearfully intense inability to

identify themselves with the mission and power of God even though, like Moses, they may have experienced miraculous God-given signs in their lives. For the servant of God to accept God's call and stand as a middleman of communication between the invisible God and visible agnostic people of this world is often intensely frustrating. This feeling may, in fact, become paralyzing in its effect upon a follower of God.

It is absolutely essential, therefore, to deal adequately with the fear which arises when the prospective evangelist becomes concerned about being a solitary witness for Christ. Many a person has never been able to gain confidence in speaking about the power of Christ because of the fear of being a solitary witness. Yet, like Moses, when one has found some support and has learned that God is faithful in accompanying his witnesses, one can often move into places and speak with people for God's sake that alone would be utterly unthinkable. Naturally, the goal of every Christian is to proceed beyond the need of supportive human companionship in order to witness. But even Christ gave his disciples the opportunity at first of going to people in pairs (see Luke 10:1), and even Paul traveled with a companion. If the task of evangelism is going to be accepted by the Christian community, it is absolutely imperative to provide an answer for the Christian's psychological feeling of aloneness in witnessing and his fear of isolated rejection.

When Moses found sufficient confidence to venture forth and communicate God's word to Pharaoh, he experienced a developing sense of the power of God in his life. To travel and camp throughout the Sinai as I have done and to reflect on what God did through Moses with the Israelites in this magnificent wilderness is a confirming reminder of the nature of God's power present in effecting his divine purposes. Moses was enabled by God's spirit to marshall a band of disgruntled slaves into a formidable group which developed very slowly in its pursuit of a God-given goal. While Moses was quick-tempered by nature, his amazing patience with the dissident Israelites—the result of his own struggles with God—became a quality in his life worthy of emulation by men and women of the twentieth century. Moreover, his love for a people that constantly seemed to exemplify a spirit of doubt carried him to the point in his passionate intercessory prayer with God that he himself was willing to be blotted out for the salvation of the sons of Israel (Exod. 32:32). Such a radical attitude of self-sacrifice must be considered to reflect the highest sense of commitment to God's work (see Paul's statement in Rom. 9:1–5). The evangelist can well learn some very significant lessons from the man who, although he was terrified to speak on behalf of God, became an extremely powerful exponent of God's will to the people of Israel.

An Evangelist's Lesson in the Numbers Game

Like Moses, Gideon (Jerubbaal, "the one who confronted Baal") found it intensely difficult to accept the call of God upon his life. Under the oak tree at Ophrah, when God summoned him to deliver Israel from Midian, Gideon's response was, "How can I do such a thing, for I am the least significant in my family and our family clan is the smallest in the tribe of Manasseh?" (Judg. 6:15). While this argument sounds strangely similar to the plea of Moses, Gideon's concern was slightly different. He wanted proof that God was actually calling him to perform such a superhuman task, and he wanted to be certain that if he responded to God's call the Lord would provide sufficient resources so that the servant would not be left "holding the bag." God's initial reply—to the effect that the opposition was weak in comparison to divine strength—was insufficient to satisfy Gideon. Gideon wanted objective proof of God's power.

But how does God deal with such doubt? More specifically, what would satisfy Gideon sufficiently, prior to the incident itself, to convince him that under God's direction the powerful Midianites would, in fact, fall before him in defeat? God broke through the natural order and sent fire to consume Gideon's sacrifice. But that event made Gideon fear death until he was assured that God's peace was with him (6:21–24). Interestingly, Gideon was only beginning the process of learning about the power and trustworthiness of God. Little did he realize that in his quest for proof from God it was not really God who was on trial but the man Gideon.

God commanded Gideon to tear down the altar of Baal and cut down the grove of immorality dedicated to Asherah. Fear of townsmen and what they might do to anyone who would demean their local deities gripped Gideon. Thus, he could mount only sufficient courage to perform the act at night (6:25–27). The night, however, scarcely hid Gideon's deed. It seems that God's servants must learn that they can seldom take a blistering stand against society's wrongs in the shadows and not expect open confrontation. In the encounter which followed, Gideon came to realize that men defend their commitments even though they may be committed to false deities like Baal. But in this event Gideon had to learn the lesson for himself that Baal was in fact powerless (6:28–32). Yet Gideon was still not ready to venture for God. Accordingly, he sought confirmation by putting out a fleece which would alternatively be both wet and dry (6:36–40). With these signs, Gideon ceased testing God.

But at this point God's test of Gideon began in earnest. The question now was: Would the servant of God be able to function on God's terms? The people of Israel responded to Gideon's summons with an army numbering thirty-two thousand. With confidence in his well-executed enlistment procedures and with the assurance of the presence of God,

Gideon was probably tasting victory before the fact. When God was finished with his servant, however, Gideon could no longer play the numbers game because he was left with less than 1 percent of his army and nothing except faith in God to face the opposition (7:1–8).

It is not uncommon for Christians to feel much like Gideon as they respond to the evangelistic commission. It is no secret that many Christians have doubts about whether God can use them and doubts about the sufficiency of God's power to bring others to Christ through them. They often find little difficulty in talking about Jesus within the context of a company of Christians or little problem in supporting evangelistic crusades. Such becomes a secure way to be involved in evangelism. But when the number of Christians becomes small, the meaning of witnessing for Jesus becomes quite evident. At such a time, faith is called to the test, and God is able to prove to the trusting servant that there can be victory for the Christian. While Gideon used his little company as effectively as possible, the victory can scarcely be attributed to Gideon's brilliance. The ancient servant of God found that it was not by might nor by power but by God's presence (see Zech. 4:6) that he was enabled to experience victory. It is equally essential for God's servant today to discover that God's work of winning the world to Christ will be accomplished only by men and women who know what it means to place their faith in God even though their resources—from man's perspective—seem to be inadequate.

An Evangelist's Lesson in Insecurity

The life of Elijah is also extremely instructive for the Christian interested in evangelism. Scarcely is there a more dynamic figure in the Old Testament than the prophet Elijah. Of the prophets who experienced firsthand the power of God, Elijah certainly must rank among the greatest. Fed by the ravens at the brook Cherith (1 Kings 17:4–6), agent for feeding a widow and her son through a never-empty jar of grain and cruse of oil (1 Kings 17:8–16), instrument for reviving a dead boy (1 Kings 17:17–24), protected by God from the king of Samaria (2 Kings 1:9–16), and delivered to heaven in a chariot of fire without rotting in a tomb (2 Kings 2:9–12), Elijah remarkably prefigures the Messiah. Indeed, Elijah was expected to return before the great and awe-filled day of the Lord's coming (Mal. 4:5).

Yet, despite these and other revelations of God's power, Elijah suffered from a sense of gripping insecurity, and he needed a reaffirmation of his call through the renewing of the perspective of God in his life. His magnificent victory on Mt. Carmel, in which fire fell from heaven upon the altar of YHWM (or Jehovah), proved unquestionably that it was he, Elijah, who was serving God and not the priests of Baal (1 Kings 18:20–39). But this great prophet, God's envoy of rain or drought, of healing or destruction, became a frightened, fleeing coward who left his home and sought refuge in the barren wastelands of the Southern Kingdom when Jezebel vowed to kill him.

It requires little imagination for most servants of God to feel the impact of words like: What is my life worth? I might as well die. I have been zealous and faithful, but now I am all alone (see 19:4, 10). At times like this, God's servants are brought to new realizations of what it means to stand between God and man. Man frequently looks for the security of God's presence and blessing through continuing earth-shattering acts of power. God surely is in control of the world no matter how bad the situation seems. But like Elijah, God's servant of today may need to learn that it is not in the smashing wind, the trembling earthquake, nor the scorching fire that the assurance of God's presence comes. As with Elijah, the voice of assurance for the Christian is usually one of quiet serenity (19:11 ff.). The active communicator of God's message who fails to understand the need for quiet confrontation with God faces the danger of drifting into improper self-centered orientations. Like Elijah, he may develop an unwholesome martyr complex or think that he stands alone as God's only faithful witness in this generation.

While powerful external acts are important confirmations of God's activity, they do not fully answer man's need of God. To be an evangelist does not mean merely being an activist for Christ. The man who witnesses on behalf of the Lord must discover a warm personal fellowship with God. The evangelist who does not know the meaning of quiet moments with God is in dire danger of becoming a self-assertive, self-sufficient empire-builder. His strengths may, indeed, become his weaknesses. Quiet encounters with the Lord are essential to prepare the servant of God for the shaking catharses of life. It is not sufficient for men to win victories or burn themselves out in the proclamation of God's Word. Because man is not God, God's servant is never beyond the need of inner strengthening.

An Evangelist's Lesson in Painful Relationships

Approximately a century after Elijah had vigorously warned Ahab and the Northern Kingdom of the increasing defilement with false deities like Baal, Hosea was called by God to an even more intensive proclamation. Unique among the writing prophets, Hosea was the only one born in the north. And with the possible exception of Jeremiah, no prophet in the Old Testament seems to have experienced greater personal anguish as a messenger of God. Indeed, so identified is Hosea with Israel's plight that his life with Gomer becomes a microcosmic copy of God's relationship with his people. To see his wife prostitute herself with other lovers and suffer the consequences of her immoral life provided Hosea with a firsthand understanding of God's agony over his faithless people.

Born out of deep personal involvement, Hosea's proclamation seems to be a model of what it means for the messenger to bridge the gap between himself and his hearers. No easy mercy is suggested here. Clearly Samaria would be required to bear its guilt (Hos. 13:16) just as Gomer suffered in slavery, but the message does not end in hopelessness. As Hosea could not leave Gomer in bondage without a second chance (3:2), so God did not reject Israel (11:8) without giving her an opportunity to return and be healed (14:1 ff.). But even more impressive than the intriguing nature of this picturesque presentation is the searching message of Hosea. One cannot help but sense that God's messenger virtually has come to embody the spirit of the self-giving God. Hosea was not an outsider preaching at sinful people; rather he was clearly identified with the sinner. The messenger, however, does not stoop to the sinner's way, and the context of loving identification with the sinner makes the stark reality of sin horribly vivid by contrast. In the manner of this magnificent prophet from the Old Covenant, the Christian who would be an effective evangelist of God's loving grace could well afford to learn the meaning of speaking to people as a caring "insider" rather than as a judgmental "outsider."

An Evangelist's Lesson in Rejection

During a subsequent era which spanned the period from the reforms of Josiah to the fall of Jerusalem, God raised in the Southern Kingdom Jeremiah, one of the most sensitive spirits in the Old Testament. The prophecies of the man from Anathoth indicate that the ebb and flow of the natural

world had left a deep impression upon him. And although
he longed for companionship, he experienced more than do
most servants of God what it means to "walk the lonesome
valley." Although he begged God for a normal life, he made
his way without a wife and family and was caustically rejected
by the citizens of his own town.

The initial response of Jeremiah to the call of God was
not unlike that of Moses. To God's election of him as a
prophet, he cried out, "Oh, Lord God! . . . I do not know
how to speak" for you. "I am barely a child" (Jer. 1:6). But
child or not, the Lord knew the integrity of his servant's
heart, and he called Jeremiah to one of the most rigorous
tasks any man of God has been commissioned to perform.

Indeed, Jeremiah's words became an impeccable standard
for Judah. When condemned by kings and priests, his message grew more intense and sounded like a clarion throughout the land (23:23 ff.). God is not honored by mere ritual,
he warned, but by the heart which is thoroughly circumcised
(7:4, 4:4). Moreover, among the prophets few struck against
idolatry and immorality with such poignant force as did
Jeremiah. Turning away from God, he announced, would
result in nothing less than making "Jerusalem a pile of ruins"
(9:11).

Sheer boldness, however, can hardly explain why Jeremiah
will always be regarded as one of the greatest prophetic voices
in the Old Covenant. His boldness on behalf of God is more
than matched by his sense of utter grief for his people. He is
their messenger of doom! Yet because of his loyalty to God
and his intense love and sensitivity for his people, he has
no hesitation in questioning God on behalf of his brethren.
The pathos of his words, "Is there no balm in Gilead?"
(8:22, RSV) have echoed throughout history. And the style
of honest argument with God, "Still, I would plead my case"
(12:1) has become an inspiration to all people who wrestle

with what seem to be insoluble problems in knowing the will of God.

But few of the people of Judah seemed to understand the dilemma which confronted this prophet. He was torn by the agony of proclaiming a message which his listeners refused to hear. He could not help but ask God why he had to speak when no one would listen. He could not help but question his role when God's people treated him as an enemy, beat him, and publicly shamed him by putting him in the stocks (20:1 ff.). Alone and helpless he cried out, "O Lord, you have seduced me" [the Hebrew is not simply *deceived* as is given in most translations] (20:7). Jeremiah cursed the day of his birth (20:14). Indeed he questioned why he was ever born (20:18). Yet his message of doom was fulfilled. He was proved correct, and he was vindicated as a true prophet according to all standards (see Deut. 18:22, Jer. 28:9). Jerusalem fell! His opponents were wrong. But even after the fall of Jerusalem, Jeremiah was not respected by most as a true prophet of Judah. Many considered him a traitor, and he was forcibly carried to Egypt by the pro-Egyptian people of Judah.

To the evangelist of today Jeremiah has much to say. It seems to be a fairly consistent human phenomenon that the proclaimers of God's word are frequently not recognized by the people of their times. The servant of God, therefore, must not expect that the word of God will always be popularly received. God's representative may instead be forced to ask with Jeremiah, "Why is my pain unceasing?" (Jer. 15:18, RSV). To stand between God and men as a communicator of God's judgment and his hope is one of the most difficult tasks in the world. God needs men and women of integrity whose goal in life is not a pat on the back or a large bank account.

God gave to the world some of the greatest insights in the Old Testament through this suffering prophet, Jeremiah.

Many of these insights could be enunciated here, but at least three need to be understood by evangelists and teachers of the Christian gospel. First, Jeremiah in his statement about prophecy provides a basis—when the Messiah finally comes—for the world-wide application of the gospel. Indeed, for interpreters of Scripture who read only the positive promises of God and fail to sense the spirit in which they were given, Jeremiah enunciates the *conditional nature of prophecy* (18:7–10). That policy statement concerning prophecy was a gigantic leap forward in man's understanding of God. Unfortunately, even today many interpreters of Scripture do not yet understand its universal significance. Whenever a prophecy is given, Jeremiah asserts, its fulfillment depends upon *obedience*. God's view to prophecy is not like words carved in stone but is built upon a living relationship with people who obey and understand his will. That is the reason God reaffirmed his covenant given to Abraham again and again with the patriarchs, priests, and kings. But where there was disobedience, God looked for someone else to carry out his purposes. How important it is for the Christian as an evangelist of today to understand that God expects obedience from his people of the New Covenant if they are to inherit the promises of God.

The second important insight from Jeremiah is that this prophet was responsible for receiving God's magnificent revelation concerning the nature of the New Covenant to be written in the hearts of God's people (31:31–34). Jeremiah understood that God planned for his people to be related to God directly and personally. Similarly, the message of a Christian evangelist must always stress the reality of the direct, personal relationship which God intends the believer to experience with the Lord.

Finally, in his own way this weeping proclaimer of God's word—centuries before the coming of the Messiah—discov-

ered that suffering is an integral part of God's relationship
to the world. This discovery virtually brought Jeremiah to
the threshold of the new era. Indeed, the life of Jeremiah
cannot help but provide strategic insight into the nature of
both proclamation and rejection for the twentieth-century
Christian whose goal is to be a fervent evangelist of the New
Covenant.

An Evangelist's Lesson in Hypocrisy [4]

The lesson from Jonah brings the discussion full circle
from Abraham. Moreover, the story of Jonah's call is the
Old Testament's most precise word about the necessity of
mission.

Jonah's reaction to the Lord's call, "Arise, go to Nineveh,"
was to find a ship going in the opposite direction. But while
he was running away from his God-appointed task, Jonah
had the seeming audacity to declare his loyalty to God—"I
am a Hebrew; and I fear the Lord, the God of heaven, who
made the sea and the dry land" (Jon. 1:9, RSV). The hypocrisy of his pious statement and the testimony of his life
collided head-on. The conclusion of Jonah 1, therefore, is an
acknowledgment that verbal affirmations and life-actions must
develop jointly.

The magnificent Hebrew poetical prayer—chapter 2, which
acknowledges the weakness of man and God's unique role in
providing salvation or deliverance—lays the foundation for
Jonah's second call. When Jonah is belched from the fish,
his reaction to the call appears to move in quite the opposite
direction from his first response. So vehemently did he preach
about the impending judgment of God and the destruction
of the hated Gentiles that the great city of Nineveh cried for
the mercy of God (3:4–9). But when God responded in mercy
to the Ninevites, Jonah became indignant. Indeed, he was

utterly incensed because he had been used as an instrument of mercy rather than as a messenger of judgment (4:1–3). There seems little doubt that Jonah detested sharing himself and the blessings of his God with these "uncircumcised dogs." Thus, although he perceived that God would be merciful to Nineveh, he nevertheless waited outside the city, hoping for its destruction.

Through the episode of the plant and the worm, however, God tried to teach Jonah the meaning of a mission of mercy (4:6–11). This book, however, concludes without a last word from Jonah. Accordingly, it leaves the reader with an existentially unanswered question: Did the servant of God really learn what it means to be called to be a communicator of God's love? That question is no less relevant for the evangelist of today. Does he or she share the blessings of the gospel only with a certain in-group? Or to state the proposition another way, do love and concern extend to people who are different? Surely God's message is not simply for one group of people. God's plan from Abraham to the present is that all the nations of the world might be blessed.

Jonah in his self-centered, nationalistic, religious pride failed miserably in his perception of God's desire to bring the world to faith. The fact that this book was received into the Old Testament canon and placed among the prophets, however, is a clear indication that some in Israel knew the destiny of God's people. But the confusion of national loyalty with the blessings of God in the context of frequent national defeat was a problem of such magnitude for Israel, that in the end Israel settled for a proselytizing pattern which could scarcely have universal appeal.

Yet inherent within the faith of Israel was the unrevoked responsibility for blessing the world. Accordingly, in the coming of Jesus, the commission to accept the responsibility for the world was reannounced. While most of Israel rejected Jesus as the Messiah and his commission, some were ready to receive both the blessing and the responsibility promised first through Abraham. Today faith in the living God through Christ Jesus has far surpassed the national limitations of the physical descendants of Abraham. And with this extension of the blessing of sonship in God has likewise passed the responsibility for reaching out to the world. The message in Jonah of proclamation beyond narrow boundaries points forward to the evangelistic dimension of the New Testament and the coming of the gospel of Christ for the whole inhabited world.

NOTES

1. In 1949 George Orwell published his highly acclaimed novel *Nineteen Eighty-Four* (New York: Harcourt, Brace & Co.) in which he warned of the dangers of a controlled society.

2. Today there seems to be greater interest among Old Testament scholars in the theology of this section of Genesis and its significance for the Jewish and Christian religions than in the mechanics of the formation of these chapters.

3. Although at first rejected, Carey's famous sermon of May 31, 1792, on Isaiah 54:2-3 and his book *An Enquiry into the Obligation of Christians to Use Means for the Conversion of the Heathen,* new facsimile edition (London: Carey Kingsgate Press, 1961) resulted in the formation of the Baptist Missionary Society on October 2, 1792.

4. The issues concerning the historical nature of Jonah should be familiar to anyone who has studied the book in detail. Those not familiar with the arguments are referred to "Old Testament introductions" such as R. K. Harrison (1969), pp. 904-18, or E. J. Young (1949), pp. 254-58, for the "historical" point of view and to R. H. Pfeiffer (1948), pp. 586-89, or A. Bentzen (1961), pp. 144-47, for the "symbolic" point of view. In terms of this study

on evangelism it is important to note that while much has been written on the historical issues, not nearly enough has been written concerning the book's exciting message. Jonah probably evidences the high point in the Old Testament in terms of Israel's responsibility for the Gentiles or the whole world.

3
Standards for Witnessing

BEHOLD THE MAN

Are you listening?

To the contemporary evangelist it is of no small importance to remember that the Greek word for "gospel" is *euaggelion*, the root of the English word *evangelism*. Moreover, the four writers of the Gospels have been called *evangelists* from the early centuries. These four New Testament evangelists were not uninvolved reporters. Their blood, toil, tears, and sweat are infused into every page of their magnificent witness. They are ambassadors for Christ who were recognized by the early Christians to have been given the special responsibility, under the guidance of the Holy Spirit, of having their testimonies about Jesus recorded as authoritative statements for all succeeding generations.

In God's wisdom he chose to allow four such testimonies to become codified among the many others which were written. Thus, contemporary Christians should not become concerned when they hear that "another gospel" has been found. New Testament scholars know of many such documents which are called Gospels. But when the four which survive in the Bible are compared with these other "gospels" the content makes it clear why the witnesses of Matthew, Mark, Luke, and John have become canonical. They were treated by the early Christians as having apostolic authority, which meant to the church that these Gospels were written by either an apostle or his assistant. They were viewed as faithful representations of Jesus and were regarded as exemplary testimonies of the meaning of his coming, his life, his death, his resurrection, and his parousia (or return).

In the second century Tatian, the intellectually astute pupil of Justin Martyr, was anxious to provide Christians with a single document which would harmonize all four Gospels. This harmonization, known as the *Diatessaron,* would have given the church a single written statement about the life and teachings of Jesus and would have removed any possible variations in the activities or the statements of Jesus recorded in the four Gospels. The preempting of the canonical Gospels by such a single document as the *Diatessaron*— another "harmony," or a written life of Jesus—has been emphatically rejected by the church throughout history. This rejection is important for all Christians to understand because each of the Gospels is more than simply a life of Christ. Each Gospel is a Spirit-directed witness concerning Jesus. Each evidences a uniqueness which is as genuinely different as is each person who seeks to be an evangelist under God. Combinations or harmonies, while helpful for comparative purposes, tend to mask the marvel of these witnesses. Therefore, it should be said that—while in the development of much of contemporary New Testament scholarship related to the Gospels there has been a rationalistic, skeptical orientation—the emphasis in current scholarship upon the unique formation of each Gospel can provide some very positive insights into the fact that each Gospel is an exciting example of what faith in Christ Jesus the Lord meant to each "evangelist."

To the contemporary reader, whose perspectives are molded by the daily newspaper habit, a word of instruction may be necessary as he approaches the Gospels. Sometimes the reader of the newspaper or the viewer of television newscasts forgets that editorializing is not confined to the editorial page or editorial comments. The delicate selection and presentation of news has an important effect upon the molding of opinion, and there is almost no such phenomenon as impartial reporting. Nevertheless, the style employed in newspapers is that of reporting facts without comments. Such

a style is regarded as giving the report an air of being un-
biased. Many readers thus assume a consequent truthfulness
in reporting. Bias and commitment are to some naïve readers
considered suspect, despite the fact that all people have presuppositions.

In the light of some popular misconceptions of the nature
of truth in written presentations, therefore, it is imperative
to understand that the Gospels are not newspaper reports.
Moreover, the evangelists make no attempt at giving an un-
committed presentation. The Gospel writers have clearly
entrusted themselves to Christ and the message of salvation.
They write from the perspective of having been made alive
in Christ, and they desire the reader to find the joy of being
drawn into the circle of God's love. The purpose of a Gospel,
then, is to present the "good news" or the gospel about new
life through Jesus. As such, it is a kind of early evangelistic
tract which was written to instruct people concerning the
implications of the coming of Christ.

The stated purpose of Luke, for instance, exemplifies the
meaning of a Gospel. While there has been considerable
discussion concerning the nature of Luke's research (Luke
1:3a) and the meaning of *akribos kathexes* (Luke 1:3b)—
whether the details are listed "in order" (KJV) or the Gospel
is an "orderly account" (RSV)—the document is not simply
a detailed historical thesis. Luke knew of many others who
were writing narratives about Jesus (1:1), but his purpose
was not simply to write a narrative. He was concerned that
the reader receive the truth (1:4) about Jesus in order that
he could make an adequate decision about the Lord. Moreover, Luke was in fact acting as a communicator on behalf
of others. The word *paradidomi* (delivered) is used by Luke
(1:2a) in the rabbinic technical sense of communicating
unchanged the message of those from whom it was received.
And those who were delivering the message should not be

considered simply reporters. They were both eyewitnesses and *ministers of the word* (1:2b). The Gospels then are communications from committed men who desire that the entire world know the life-altering truth about Jesus Christ.

Each New Testament evangelist or Gospel writer has his own way of telling the story about Jesus. Each employs the pericopes (units from the life of Jesus) in the way he believes they can be most forcefully presented. Under the guidance of the Holy Spirit, each has become a powerful agent for bringing the world to acknowledge Jesus as Savior and Lord.

An understanding of the formation and purpose of a Gospel can be gained through a confrontation with two models. Mark represents the Synoptic tradition (Matthew, Mark, and Luke). In organization it differs slightly from Matthew and Luke, but it has sufficient similarities that if one reads a thorough introduction he should be able to formulate the unique witness of the two other Synoptic Gospels. John is a different kind of witness and also needs to receive the attention of evangelists.

Revealing a Secret

The first of the evangelistic tracts (canonical Gospels) to be written about Jesus apparently came from the pen of John Mark.[1] His report of Jesus was probably intended for the evangelization of the Romans. To these robust people Mark spells out a brief, vigorous, and realistic portrayal of Jesus. The genealogy, birth, and Israelitic friendships of the servant of God—important for Matthew and Jewish readers— scarcely would have been significant to the world rulers of the day. They are, thus, absent from his witness. Moreover, by comparison with the others, little concerning the teachings of Jesus is presented in this shortest of the Gospels. For the philosophic-loving Greeks to whom Luke was writing, such an emphasis would be important. For the Romans the major facts and the primary significance aroused immediate interest. Thus, to the people of action Mark reveals that Jesus is their ideal. Even in the use of action-oriented words Mark has his readers in mind. For example, the word *straightway* or *immediately* occurs forty-two times in this short book.

While this Gospel has been outlined by Christian scholars in many ways, there seems no doubt to me that a major change of emphasis occurs at the story of Peter's confession in Caesarea Philippi (8:27 ff.). To those interested in the work of evangelism, this shift is of vital significance. That such a confession seems to divide the Gospel immediately ought to suggest something concerning Mark's purpose—his desire to bring the reader to know and confess Jesus. Clearly it is from the role which this story of Caesarea plays in the Gospel that the genius of Mark as an evangelistic writer is most clearly viewed.

Prior to this confessional pericope (story), Mark's basic concern is to reveal to the world who Jesus is. He does this very effectively by showing how the disciples seek to cope with the call to discipleship—a matter by no means irrelevant to the contemporary evangelist. Thus, following the initial summons of the various disciples (1:17–18, 20; 2:14; 3:13–19; see also 2:17), Mark indicates the functions of the twelve: (1) they are sent to preach, and (2) they are given authority to cast out demons (3:14). Then, their general education concerning Jesus is begun. They are present at the time when parables are taught, but they are also privately instructed in the meanings of these parables (4:1–34; see especially vv. 33–34). They are awed by the miraculous power of Jesus, and they question how he can perform these great acts (4:35–

5:54; see especially 4:41). Nevertheless, they also witness the strange absence of miracles in Jesus' hometown. Jesus indicates that the reason is the result of unbelief (6:1–6).

Then, the disciples themselves are sent without physical supplies to begin their tasks—to preach repentance and to cast out demons (6:7–13, 30). By this time their preparation should have been completed. Yet, when put to the test, the disciples really fail to understand who Jesus is because they do not see beyond his powerful works (6:51–52; 8:17–21). They are like people who have been associated with Christianity and who have sensed the strange power of God present in the church; yet since such an association with Christianity has not become a living part of them, they are unable to pass beyond intellectualizing about Jesus. Accordingly, they have difficulty relating personally to the power of God and the person of Christ. It seems rather significant that given all their experiences the disciples at this point were still primarily just spectators.

But following immediately after a rather telling story of a blind man receiving sight (8:22–25), Mark seems to set Caesarea symbolically as the first major breakthrough for the disciples. In answer to the question of Jesus, "Who do you say that I am?" Peter on behalf of the twelve responds, "You are the Christ [the Messiah]" (Mark 8:29, RSV).[2] This confession marks a moment of change. It is a crossing-point or the place of a new beginning in the life of a person. If one recalls Mark's Gospel-plan, this confession is in fact Mark's starting point or the presupposition for his entire Gospel. It should be remembered that he initiates this witness with the affirmation, "The beginning of the gospel of Jesus Christ, the Son of God" (1:1, RSV). While Peter did not yet fully understand what he said at Caesarea, *Mark did!* And every evangelist who follows in the footsteps of Mark must also understand the nature of confessing Jesus as the Christ, the one who indeed is the Son of God.

Mark is committed to the fact that Jesus is God's promised one, and Mark's purpose is to bring the reader to an understanding of the reason for the coming of this Messiah or Christ. He knows, however, that faith in Jesus Christ is a mysterious, God-given miracle. Accordingly, his selection of the Lord's parables point in the same direction. Jesus taught that there are various types of soil which receive seed (just as there are various people who hear the gospel), but only one type is really productive (4:10-20). Moreover, faith —like a young plant—is in the beginning difficult to recognize, but in the end there is no doubt about its validity (4:26-29, 30-32). Clearly, for Mark, the reality of faith and the significance of confession are of paramount importance. At Caesarea with the breakthrough of the disciples, there is no longer a need to question the power of Jesus or who he is. The questions, therefore, are changed. Thereafter, the concern is with Christ's purpose in coming to earth.

This desire of Mark to clarify the need for an authentic faith and a legitimate confession reaches to the heart of this Gospel. Many scholars have been perplexed by what Wilhelm Wrede in 1903 [3] identified as the "messianic secret." Why does Jesus warn the demons not to speak concerning him (see 1:34; 3:11-12)? Why in the beginning does he also charge his disciples to silence (5:43)? That the silence was not kept either by the demons or the disciples is clear. Why then did Mark record these statements? Some scholars like Bultmann employ such a phenomenon to suggest that Mark misunderstood the person and role of Jesus, namely, Jesus was not in fact the messianic Son of God. Thus, similar to Bultmann, some divide Jesus Christ into the Jesus of Nazareth (a human) and the Christ of the Christian's faith (the

God of encounter). Accordingly, the messianic secret tends to be used to support the nondeity of Jesus. While the issue is complex, in my opinion Mark is trying to communicate something of great significance by this means. The answer, it seems, is in the nature of witnessing, and the importance of Mark's organization ought certainly to be understood by every evangelist.

Anyone can speak about Jesus. Such is the unquestioned perspective of Mark. Even devils and misguided disciples can open their mouths. *They speak when they should not because they know not the reality concerning that which they speak.* But authentic witnesses of Jesus are different. They have an understanding of Christ's coming which goes beyond words.

Almost like a mystery novel, Mark organizes the clues concerning his understanding of witnessing. At Caesarea, immediately following Peter's confession, Jesus again gave the warning to silence (8:30). But the situation was changing. Jesus began at this point to unfold to the disciples that he must suffer, be killed, and rise again. Such an idea of a suffering Messiah was totally unwelcomed by the disciples, and Peter, on their behalf, voiced his strong opposition (8:31–32).

Immediately after this Caesarea exchange, Mark reports the story of the transfiguration. The disciples are again warned, but this time the warning is altered ever so slightly. But for the one who understands, the change is telling. At this point the disciples are charged to refrain from witnessing—"until after the resurrection" (9:9). The significance of the resurrection for evangelism is profound.

The disciples and Mark's readers are thus warned that they must learn the meaning of the crucifixion and resurrection if they are to be effective witnesses. Interestingly, both in terms of length of the Gospel and purpose for which it was written, Mark's message remains only half-completed at Caesarea. In writing this testimony Mark is a postresurrection Christian. He is convinced that Jesus is alive. He clearly believes in the death and resurrection of Christ, and he realizes that an authentic witness is impossible without a commitment to the risen Jesus. But the cross stands between the disciples and the powerful proclamation of the good news.

From Caesarea Philippi forward, therefore, the ministry of Jesus is explained in terms of the cross. Although Mark realized that the way of the cross would be unwelcome to his readers, he also knew it was rejected at first by the disciples. They needed to learn a new style of life—the way of servanthood. Both for the Roman readers of Mark's day as well as for the contemporary citizen of the Western world, this menial, dependency perspective is viewed as undesirable. Yet it is not a perspective that makes man weak. It shows man who he really is and allows him to find the power of God.

The disciples could not heal the demoniac boy because they did not understand the real meaning of prayer (9:14–29). They were selfish and forbade others to do works in the name of Jesus (9:38–41). As misguided authoritarians they rejected children (10:13–16) because they had to learn the nature of God's marvelous, encompassing grace. They wanted the chief seats in God's kingdom because they could not fathom the way of ministry and the nature of servanthood (10:35–45). But through their denials (14:27–31, 50–52, 66–72) and in the process of watching the events leading to the crucifixion (see 15:40–41), they learned the meaning of the *broken way of the cross.*

Moreover, with the awe-filled experience of the resurrection they began to look back, to understand the reason for the coming of Jesus, and to perceive the unbelievable fact of the incarnation. This affirmation of the incarnation has been central to historic Christianity. To be an evangelist without such a confession is to be adrift in a shoreless "Christian" sea. Mark affirms his confession of the incarnation in a unique manner as he consciously juxtaposes Jesus' self-designation "Son of man" with his own confessional designation "Son of God." Thereby, he challenges the reader to discover for himself the magnificent reality of the good news or gospel, namely, the meaning of the Son of man who was actually the Son of God.

This gospel is not to be identified with some vague words about new life or judgment or ethical standards. Again, the pericope at Caesarea provides insight for today's evangelist by identifying the gospel. At Caesarea Jesus says, "Whoever loses his life for *my sake* and the *gospel's* will save it" (8:35, RSV, italics mine; see also 10:29). The content of the gospel is Jesus, and evangelism is witnessing about Jesus.

In this existential age, when much witnessing is concentrated upon personal subjective experience and testimonies run ad nauseam concerning the former sinful life of Christians, the meaning of evangelism needs clearly to be recognized. A Christian testimony is only an adequate testimony when it *highlights Jesus*. When it majors upon one's former life or on one's self, it is sub-Christian. There was no question from Mark's point of view as to the meaning of *euaggelion*. For this reason he opens his magnificent work with the unambiguous words concerning "the gospel of Jesus Christ, the Son of God."

The church of Jesus Christ today is greatly indebted to the man John Mark who, at such an early point in history following our Lord's resurrection, accepted the task of setting down in writing a forceful evangelistic testimony concerning Jesus. Moreover, he isolated clearly the task of Christ's disciples—proclamation which leads men to repentance, and implementation of the power of God to dispel the forces of the devil. Finally, by so effectively enveloping the disciples' task in the spirit of suffering love, Mark's witness to the Lord has become a model for evangelists of Jesus throughout the world.

Sign for Believing [4]

The purpose of the Fourth Gospel is made eminently clear in Chapter 20.

Now, indeed, Jesus did many other signs in the presence of his disciples which are not recorded in this book; but these have been written in order that you may believe that Jesus is the Christ, the Son of God; and that believing you might have life in his name (John 20:30–31).

From early Christian history, the Book of John was viewed by Christians as somewhat diffeerent than the other Gospels, and therefore it became known as "the spiritual Gospel." In reflecting on the meaning of this designation and the purpose for which John was written, it seems that the theological implications of the coming of Christ have been spelled out in greater detail in this evangelistic tract than in its Synoptic counterparts. The prospective evangelist, however, should not assume that non-Christians and new converts will find this tract easy to understand. While it has some marvelous verses like John 3:16, the symbolism such as "eating the flesh of the Son of man" (6:53) may be just as difficult for the uninitiated to comprehend as it was for the early Jews. But the amazing feature of this Gospel is that it soon finds a special place in the heart of a new believer, while it stretches the mind and life of the most mature Christian. Moreover, the stories are so insightful that they frequently contain, not merely the message of life, but also perceptive implications concerning the nature and style of evangelism. The book opens with a prologue in which the coming and reception of Jesus are reviewed. To believe, receive, or to know Jesus is perhaps the basic premise from which the Christian evangelist operates. This principle having been stated, however, it must be admitted that true believing seems to take its position between two counterfeits—a confession of orthodox "beliefs" without "meeting" God and a subjective experience which has little contact with believing, Christian obedience. Most Christians would affirm the necessity of avoiding both extremes. It must be recognized, however, that practice has not always been as good as teaching. Some perspective on this problem may be found in the prologue.

When one speaks of "believing" in the Book of John, the verse which usually comes immediately to mind is: "But as many as received him, to them gave he power to become the sons of God, *even* to them that believe on his name" (John 1:12, KJV, italics mine). Interestingly, when many people quote this verse they stress the word *even*, which seems to imply that the minimum "belief" is to believe in the name of Jesus. To stress the word *even*, however, is unfortunate because the word does not appear in the Greek text. But that translational situation is not the only problem. To treat believing in the name of Jesus as a "belief" leads to a basic misunderstanding of the Fourth Gospel. Throughout this book John carefully avoids using the Greek noun for "faith" or "belief" as well as the noun for "knowledge." Instead, he uses the verbs! This fact is extremely significant because early within the church's life a movement began to grow which stressed knowledge and beliefs of heavenly secrets. This movement was a primitive stage of the Gnostic heresy.

John was undoubtedly determined that all his readers realize that it is not *what* you know and believe but *whom* you know and believe that is the basis of Christianity. It is absolutely imperative for the Christian evangelist to understand this distinction because to instruct or catechize a person does not necessarily result in the impartation of new life!

The story of Martha in the raising of Lazarus is very helpful on this point. Martha reports that because of Jesus' absence her brother died. Jesus replies, "Your brother will
rise." In effect Martha's answer was, "Oh yes, Lord, I know
a little general theology. I am sure that my brother will rise
at the resurrection." Then Jesus says, "Martha, I am the
resurrection and the life" (11:25). These significant words
mean that the very essence of life, a quality of God alone,
was somehow present in a person that walked the earth.
Was Martha ready for that kind of a statement? Seemingly
she was because when Jesus asked her, "Do you believe this?"
her answer was, "Of course, Lord; I believe that you are the
Christ, the Son of God, the one who is coming into the
world." With this statement the conversation between Jesus
and Martha temporarily ceases, and she proceeds to go and
tell Mary that Jesus has arrived.

The entire process starts over again—if only Jesus had
been present! After a sorrowful movement of his inner spirit
over their unbelief, similar to that when from the hill he
gazes at the unreceptive Jerusalem (Matt. 23:37), Jesus goes
to the tomb and tells them to take away the stone. Notice
the one who speaks out at this point. It is Martha! And she
says, "Lord, he has been in the tomb four days and he already stinks" (11:39). Clearly, she is the same Martha who
had just previously said, "Of course, Lord; I believe." In
fact, she also said, "I know that whatever you ask from God,
he will give it to you" (11:22). The point of this story is that
the relationship between verbal affirmation and life commitment may not be as close as many Christians assume.
Accordingly, the evangelist must be thorough in his proclamation and realistic in dealing with the commitments of
people. New life in Christ is more than words.

The evangelist reading the Fourth Gospel should also be
constantly aware of the fact that the coming of Jesus de-

mands honest decision and thus sets man in one of two basic
categories with God. Even in the first chapter, John tells us
that Jesus came to his own creation, but his own creatures
did not receive him (1:11). This rejection of the love of God
is the tragic stance of man that drives him to face God's
judgment.

Perhaps the most penetrating discussion of judgment is
expressed in chapter 3, which contains one of the Bible's
best-known verses—the great enunciation of God's love
(3:16). The context concerns a discussion between Jesus and
Nicodemus. Nicodemus begins with a rather superficial
greeting, "We know you are a teacher sent by God." The
evangelist should note the style of Jesus here because he
wastes no time with such formalities. Instead, he shows Nicodemus that although he is a member of the Sanhedrin—the
Jewish council—he does not even begin to know what the
teachings of Jesus really mean. This teacher from God comes
to bring life. He does not come simply to impart wisdom or
interesting styles of logic for Jewish lawyers. His purpose is
to bring man to the point of decision! As the serpent which
was erected by Moses in the wilderness became a symbol of
both mercy and judgment, so the lifting up of Jesus is to
become the vehicle for both grace and condemnation—life
for those who accept but death for those who refuse God in
Christ.

The great motive of God in Jesus, however, is not condemnation. Jesus came into the world to bring the world
to wholeness (3:17). God's love (3:16) has never been a
matter of deception or play acting. In the coming of Jesus,
God was absolutely serious. This unmitigated seriousness
confronts man with his most significant choice. Every other
choice is secondary. In the context of life decision, therefore,
these words sound like thunder: "The one who trusts him is
not condemned; the one who does not trust stands already

condemned" (3:18). And lest anyone could yet mistake the meaning of Jesus' coming, John concludes his piercing third chapter with: "The one who trusts the Son has life eternal, but the one who refuses to trust the Son shall not catch sight of life, for the judgment of God rests upon him" (3:36).

Why does judgment appear so harsh in this chapter which is regarded as the great chapter of love? It seems that only in the light of God's amazing love can the rejection of his son be seen in its severity. Indeed, judgment and salvation are harmonized in God's gospel. Thus, the preaching of salvation as a universalism (that ultimately all will be saved) is a superficial proclamation of the good news. To treat man's decisions in the world as meaningless in sight of God is to make God as spineless as men and to regard God's active love as senseless.

Because for John the rejection of Jesus is of ultimate significance, the cleansing of the temple (chap. 2) becomes vital to John's presentation of the gospel. Inadequate, self-centered worship is absolutely rejected when found among God's people. Places of worship are built for communion between God and his people. The misuse of worship centers and worship practices for man's own ends brings only the condemnation of God. As John indicates, Jesus is not fooled by the nature of man's commitment (2:23-25). He realizes the inner attachments of man, and he knows that what is central in man's believing will be reflected in the way man worships.

The story of the Samaritan woman (chap. 4) is an excellent example of the understanding of Jesus. When the woman responds to the Lord's request for a drink, one receives the distinct impression that she is probing to find out what kind of man Jesus is. Her relationship with men was quite obvious. The reply of Jesus concerning living water evokes a materialistic answer that she would be delighted to have such a spring so that she could stop the drudgery of fetching water from the well, especially in the heat of the day when the other women of the town did not need to come.

The next moves on the part of Jesus and the woman form a prize example of evangelistic technique. Jesus tells her to call her husband, to which she responds, "I do not have a husband." When Jesus tells her the nature of her sinful life, she tries a stunt which is familiar to all witnesses of the gospel as a discussion moves close to the sinful life-motivations of a person. The attempt is to get the witness off on a tangential argument concerning which is the right church or place to worship (4:20). Jesus hardly falls for a side-tracking discussion. His answer to the woman is that buildings and places are secondary and the relationship to God is primary. Not to be outdone the woman tries again, and this time with another familiar move—the eschatological argument. But Jesus' answer is that for the woman the eschatological moment of decision has arrived.

At this point the woman departs, convinced that she has met the messenger from God who could make the difference in her life, and she joyously shares the knowledge of meeting Christ with others. Her comment to the men is very revealing: "Come, see a man who told me everything which I ever did" (4:29). Undoubtedly, Jesus did not do that, but he spoke to her concerning the important sinful practices of her life. She knew that if he understood these matters he knew about her entire life.

Such an encounter with Christ cannot help but bring a person to the point of decision. An evangelist's privilege today is to be a vehicle for enabling such a decisive life-encounter. But the evangelist must be careful lest he stumble into argumentative pitfalls and never arrive at the point where the non-Christian encounters Christ and reaches the point of decision.

This role of the Christian evangelist in bringing people to the moment of decision with Christ is rooted in Jesus' view of his ministry. He stated this view forcefully when he said of himself, "For the purpose of judgment I entered this world in order that those who do not see might see and those who see might become blind" (9:39). Throughout this Gospel judgment is regarded, not simply as a far-off event related only to the *eschaton* (last day), but as already having begun with the crucifixion and resurrection. Never to be forgotten are the words, "Now is the judgment of this world, now shall the prince of this world be cast out" (12:31).

The cross and the resurrection stand together as the great dividing rod of mankind. From that point, intensity of life with God finds its new beginning. True life begins with a decision for God, and such a decision means taking a stand in the world of conformity. This stand may mean rejection and persecution, but Jesus recognized the probability of such a reaction. He did not expect the life of his followers to be easy, but he charged them to remember that in him they would find their true peace and security. In the world they would have tribulation; "but be confident," he said, "I have conquered the world!" (16:33).

In keeping with John's purpose that signs were given to encourage believing and commitment to Jesus, this Gospel-tract has often been referred to as a book of signs. In interpreting the idea of signs, it is important for the contemporary evangelist to recognize that a sign is not simply to be viewed as a miracle. It is, instead, an evangelistic phenomenon which points beyond itself to the need for understanding and accepting Jesus, the Christ.

The first sign in this Gospel occurs at Cana where water is turned into wine. Parenthetically, it should be noted that the translators of the King James Version cause confusion because they render the Greek *semion* meaning "sign" as

"miracle" here (2:11) and elsewhere, while they translate it
correctly in John 20:30. The result of these mixed transla-
tions is that many readers fail to grasp the significance of the
Johannine signs and thus fail to discover the meaning of the
first sign. The importance of this sign is seemingly not that
Jesus sanctified marriage. Nor is it likely that he was handing
down his verdict on alcohol. The significance is that somehow in changing six large pots of water into wine Jesus manifested his glory, and the disciples were aroused to trust him
(2:11). In this act the disciples became aware that Jesus was
not like any other leader—not even John the Baptizer.
Moreover, Jesus was not subject to influence—not even the
influence of his mother. Instead, he was motivated by something which led him quite consciously to a determined hour
(2:4)—the hour of his death and resurrection. Accordingly,
because of the perspective it provides, this seemingly insignificant act is called by John the *archē* (initial guide, 2:11)
to the signs of Jesus. This sign, like an evangelistic call,
challenges persons to trust in the God-man.

The healing of the man at the pool (John 5) provides
further insight into this Jesus who summons men and women
to follow him. For thirty-eight years a paralyzed man waited
for the heaven to open and a miraculous healing event to
occur. But all Jesus did was to say to the crippled man, "Get
up, roll up your bed, and be on your way" (5:8). This act was
not the kind of magic of which a sick man might dream.
These were mere words. But how could such power be in
words? Who was this Jesus? John must have viewed this sick
man as a symbol of Judaism. Both waited with their pet
theories—the man with his theories of healing, the Jews with
their theories of the coming of the Messiah. One of the Jews'
main theories was that the Messiah would come when Israel
kept perfectly one Sabbath. But this Jesus healed on the
Sabbath. How could he be the Messiah? And there was here

an additional problem because Jesus calls God his personal father. From fear of taking God's name in vain, the Jews had ceased to use his name. But Jesus calls God his father! According to Jewish thought of the day, this act was undoubtedly blasphemy.

The Jews, thus, refused to accept Christ's healing as God-directed because of their theories. Yet true healing comes only from God. Sadly, men's little rules often blind them to the work of God. Twice Jesus challenges them: "Wake up! Realize that the Son does nothing on his own" (5:19, 30). But the Jews with their theories would not listen. Similarly, it should not come as a surprise to the evangelist of today when confronting people with the message of eternal life that they clutch their self-oriented theories and reject the proclamation. Jesus reminded his disciples that the servant is not greater than the Master (13:16).

Not only do people generally not accept a witness, but the evangelist will frequently feel the pulse of hostility and sense the alienation and withdrawal of interest when the implications of the message become clearer. Such is the case presented in connection with the sign inherent in the feeding of the five thousand (John 6). In this story John supplies his readers with one of the most significant statements in the Gospel related to the signs. Jesus says, "You seek me, not because you saw signs, but because you ate of the bread and you became full" (6:26). At this point the King James Version again ineptly renders *semion* as "miracle." Contrary to the King James Version, however, the people saw miracles, and that is exactly why they followed Jesus. But while the people ate bread and saw the miracle, they did not understand the significance of the bread or in fact see the sign.

This difference between miracle and sign becomes more intense when Jesus affirms that while in the wilderness their fathers ate manna but died (6:49), yet those who eat this bread which descends from heaven (6:50), namely, Jesus (6:51), shall live forever. The Jews had waited expectantly for their deliverer. They thought a new Moses might come (see Deut. 18:15; John 1:21), but when the sign of the new Moses was given, they did not see it (6:29–32). They requested, instead, a continual supply of bread (6:34). It is pathetic, indeed, that mankind misses the hope for which it awaits because the answer is too rigorous and does not fit man's self-conceived formulas. The pseudodisciple is unwilling to follow because something is demanded which is beyond his desired commitment. At such times, however, the real follower of Jesus continues when the interested adherent drifts to other attachments that require less by way of personal commitment (6:66–69).

With subsequent meetings the situation between Jesus and the Jews becomes even more intense. In John 8:12 and the following verses, Jesus stands before the multitude and proclaims, "I am the light of the world." This affirmation begins one of the most intriguing encounters in this Gospel. The result of the discussion is that the Jews are unable to accept the truth presented by Jesus. The reason for their nonacceptance, Jesus avers, is their lack of a close relationship with God. While they argue that they are sons of Abraham and free to respond to God, Jesus concludes that their anger, hostility, and murderous inclinations indicate that they are in actuality sons of the devil (8:44).

As though John senses that his readers might react unfavorably to such a forthright judgment, he follows the conversation with a lucid sign. A man born blind is actually made by Jesus to see, and when the Jews find out what has occurred, they admonish the man to "give God the praise," but they inform him "we know that this man [Jesus] is a sinner" (9:24, RSV). The man answers to the effect, "I don't know what he is, but I know I can see." The Jews, however,

refuse to accept his word and thus reveal their basic problem. Even though they call witnesses—who affirm the blind
man's blindness—and they are faced with the fact of a man
who has been cured, they are unable to accept the fact as fact
because of their presuppositions. Accordingly, their only alternative (9:34) is to call the man a degrading name (thus
stigmatizing him) and to excommunicate him (thus closing
their eyes to the real situation).

It is no surprise, therefore, that when Lazarus is raised
from the dead, the Jewish leadership considers itself backed
into a corner. They recognize the nature of the signs of Jesus
but clearly deny their validity. Their decision is that Jesus
must die or they will be destroyed. But this death of one
man for the nation (11:50) is, according to the Fourth Gospel, the greatest sign of all.

The final days of Jesus' life are for John the most significant, and his record of these days is one of the most dramatic pieces of literature. To many, however, the words
have long since ceased to raise excitement. The drama of the
real murder or execution of the Son of God and of the unbelievable God-empowered resurrection seems to have faded
like a dream. Moreover, the fanciful longing of most minds
for a happy ending to every unhappy story seems to cloud
the reality of the resurrection. The almost universal testimony of the church's lack of understanding for the resurrection is its general failure to proclaim it, except on Easter
when it is cluttered with effeminate lilies. The passion or
the death of Jesus has become the primary element of the
Western church's proclamation, and the resurrection has
frequently been severed from its rightful place alongside the
passion. If the church has failed to convince the world of the
joy of Christianity, perhaps part of the reason is that it has
severely truncated its own message. In view of this fragmentation which has often characterized the church's evan-

gelistic proclamation, it is important to remember that John wrote his Gospel after both the passion and the resurrection and that he treats the events of these last days as a unit.

The first of the great Passion Week events is remembered on Maundy Thursday. For those of nonliturgical traditions, the expression Maundy Thursday usually carries little significance except that it is the day that precedes Black Friday. The word *maundy*, however, is a defective derivative from the Latin verb *mando*, "I command." Significantly, therefore, it is not the betrayal or the last supper but a commandment which the church commemorates by this day. In so doing the church spotlights John's selection of the final events. John says almost nothing of that portion of the last meal which became the prototype of the church's communion service. Instead, he includes a captivating episode of humility in which Jesus washes the disciples' feet (John 13).

This incident reaches its climax when Jesus delivers to his disciples the new commandment of love (13:34). Judas has been dismissed (13:30), and in the last few moments of his last meal, Jesus sets before his little band the quality which was most to epitomize his followers. Nothing is more needed for the twentieth-century church than to remember that *a Christian is characterized by love* (13:35)! Moreover, the evangelist who seeks to proclaim Christ without a deep sense of love is misrepresenting the message of God.

In the next four chapters John strategically sets down Jesus' magnificent concluding remarks. The Christian receives the great promise (chap. 14) that Jesus has prepared for him a destiny (14:1 ff.) and that in the present era he is not left to his own resources (14:18). Then follows (chap. 15) the promise of abundant joy for the believer when he, as the branch, is nurtured directly from Christ. Next, (chap. 16) the place of the believer in a hostile world is discussed. Finally, (chap. 17) there is recorded what may be the Bible's greatest prayer.

Perhaps no chapter of the Bible has furnished a greater basis for the modern spirit of ecumenism than this prayer. Yet ecumenism can be a hollow wish unless the church remembers the basis for its oneness—"that the world may believe that you [Father] sent me" (17:21). While ecumenical or cooperative emphases are evident among almost all groups of Christians, whatever their theological conviction, the center of all such Christian action and discussion must be the evangelistic mission of the church. Where this evangelistic task fails to form the core of the church's ecumenical interest, the results wll ultimately bring a greater fragmentation. Let the true *evangelistic* mission of the church, therefore, guide each denomination of the Christian faith in a careful evaluation of how the ecumenical spirit is manifested among them because the church is committed to take the prayer of Christ seriously!

The dramatic arrest, trial, and crucifixion of Jesus are next presented. Interestingly, John omits the incident of the famous kiss of death. Instead, he focuses upon the contrast between the seemingly weak Jesus who needs no weapons—not even Peter's sword (18:10–11a)—and the pseudostrong band which comes out to seize him "armed to the teeth" (18:2–9, 11b–12). The swift trials which mock justice and the dramatic denials of Peter which culminate in the crow of the cock provide a most fitting introduction to the grim execution of Jesus. In the light of centuries of theological debate and varying sermonic presentations, it is often necessary for the believer to remind himself that Jesus died a real death, bled actual blood, and was buried in a genuine tomb. Yet, if our Gospel ended at that point, it is probable that *there would be no gospel, no church, and no Christianity!*

Christianity is established upon the resurrection. To treat it as insignificant, to regard it as a religious myth, or to deny it is in effect to relegate Christianity to the commonness of teachings and opinions found elsewhere in other religions. Christianity is a religion based upon the witness of the actual death and resurrection of Jesus.

Among the witnesses of these facts, John has selected for special mention the testimony of Thomas (20:26 ff.). It is strange how time has played cruelly with Thomas because he is best remembered as the doubter. If Thomas was a doubter, he certainly was not a coward because it was he who announced his willingness to die with the Lord (11:16). Probably a very practical man, Thomas realized what it meant to enter hostile Judea before Christ's death and what it might mean if there was a real resurrection. For men like Thomas the church must be forever grateful because Christianity stands upon a witness such as Thomas who refused to be convinced unless he saw for himself. After he became convinced that Jesus was alive, Thomas tendered Christianity's greatest confession about Jesus—"My Lord and my God." When Jesus replied, "Because you have seen me you have believed," in effect he affirmed that Thomas has set the standard of confession based upon seeing. For future generations he added, "Blessed are those who follow in your footsteps even though they have not seen me."

Originally, John closed his Gospel with this confession and the statement of his purpose, but he later added a significant appendix (chap. 21). Something was left unsaid. Three times Peter had denied Jesus. Three times the Lord now searched Peter's commitment. The crushing significance of Christ's question impressed itself indelibly upon Peter so that even his First Epistle echoes this commission (1 Pet. 5:2). But Peter was still Peter. Inconsistent at Caesarea where he is called both "rock" and "Satan" (Matt. 16:17–23); here, while he receives his personal commission, he seems more concerned about the commission of another. How typical of the Christian church! But to inconsistent Peter and to each of us as Christians the risen Lord gives a continuing word: Concern yourself not with the discipleship of another. You . . . follow me (see John 21:22)! Whether such discipleship means death or long life, the disciple is called to the task of extending the kingdom of God so that all the world may have the opportunity of knowing the infinite God who so loved the people of the world that he sent his only son Jesus to die for their sins and raised him again for their salvation.

This message of the marvelous loving concern of God expressed in the life and work of Christ is infused throughout the four New Testament Gospels. These Gospels are succinctly written testimonies from the pens of authoritative representatives in the early church. Their witnesses have formed for the contemporary church the uniquely accepted standards of proclamation concerning the Lord Jesus. Moreover, they are the means for insuring that Christian faith is rooted, not in mere subjective experience, but in a relationship with the historically proclaimed Jesus Christ who effected the possibility of genuine new life for mankind.

Whenever human beings discover for themselves the reality of this crucified, risen Christ, personal life-changing revolutions begin. So startling were the earliest revolutions that the Christians in the Book of Acts were referred to as people who turned the world upside down. To bear an authentic witness concerning Jesus, therefore, is to participate in man's greatest revolution, the earliest record of which is the next dramatic subject in the biblical study of evangelism.

NOTES

1. While his name does not appear in the Gospel, his identification was recorded in the second century by Papias and preserved by the church historian Eusebius.

2. Some ancient Greek manuscripts add "the Son of God."

3. The book was finally translated into English in 1971 by J. C. G. Greig as *The Messianic Secret* (Cambridge: James Clarke & Co.).

4. Some of the ideas in this section have been enunciated in my earlier work *Great Themes from John*, © Gerald L. Borchert 1965–66.

4

Turning the World Upside Down

TURNING THE WORLD UPSIDE DOWN

Scarcely is there a more exciting record concerning the church's evangelistic task than the Book of Acts. In the twenty-eight chapters of this treatise, expectation of Christian believers is wedded to the powerful response of God's action in such a way that the reader who scans the book centuries after its writing is drawn into the pulsating sphere of a church come alive through the work of the Holy Spirit. To study the Book of Acts, therefore, can be for the Christian one of his most rewarding experiences. To recover for the twentieth-century church the dynamic life expressed in that book ought to be each Christian's earnest prayer.

Whether the Christian's faith is simplistic or mature, the uncluttered simple trust in the power of God's activity evident in men who seemingly "turn the world upside down" (Acts 17:6) challenges the contemporary Christian to discover for himself the nature of a flaming commitment to God. To be persecuted and driven from one's place of residence and yet continue avid in witnessing to God's work in Christ Jesus may seem like a strange tale to the comfort-loving Christian of today's Western world. But the contemporary Western Christian who steeps himself in the Book of Acts senses with growing uneasiness that Paul may have been dead right when he preached that "through many tribulations we must enter the kingdom of God" (14:22, RSV). Hardly does one pray for tribulation, but scarcely should the serious Christian witness expect to escape its claws. To fear God rather than men and pray for courage to witness in all circumstances (4:19–20, 29–30) is a basic presupposition of Luke, the writer of the Acts of the Apostles.

The Book of Acts has received significant attention from scholars. Some have considered it a patchwork of theological affirmations reflecting not historical incidents but dogmatic conceptions which gave birth to the recorded narratives or provided the basis for remolding historical incidents into an acceptable theological framework. In this process the speeches of Acts have been compared with speeches in the works of Greek historians, and the result is an evaluation that the speeches are not authentic but are conceptualized in the mind of the writer of Acts. With this skepticism concerning the historical basis for the book has gone a late dating and a rejection of Luke as the author. F. C. Baur[1] of Tübingen, the most famous critic of Acts, writing in the first half of the nineteenth century, regards the book as a second-century political document which sought to synthesize radical differences between early Hebraic and early Hellenistic Christianity. His skeptical views have made an indelible impression upon scholarship, and the ghost of Baur still lurks in many works today.

Fortunately for Acts, around the turn of the twentieth century Sir William Ramsay began to visit the sites mentioned in Acts, and this advocate of the Tübingen hypothesis completely reversed his position in favor of the reliability of Luke as a historian. One by one the affirmations of Baur's theory have been scrutinized by later scholars and found indefensible, but unfortunately this does not mean that skepticism over the Book of Acts has been laid to rest.

Perhaps the reason for the continuing skepticism lies in the very nature of the book itself. Its forthright challenge to evangelism and its record of a seemingly absolute and unsophisticated reliance upon the power of God is a hard message for the twentieth century to accept. It is not only some scholars who seek to dismiss the implication of this book, but many church people frequently regard the stories with a kind of fairy-tale air, perhaps applicable to the first century but strangely out of tune today. To turn to this early Christian document, therefore, and actually listen to its message is a crucial experience for anyone who would follow in the evangelistic train of the apostles.

Obviously, the Acts cannot quite be considered as a record of early church history. From one point of view it is a limited catalog of events. Little is said concerning the movement of Christianity into Egypt and Africa or eastward into Mesopotamia. It is a selected history which in the first half concerns the church in Palestine and concentrates primarily upon the mission of Peter. The second half concerns the expansion of the church to the Greco-Roman world, ending at Rome itself, and concentrates upon the mission of Paul. The development of the book follows roughly the order suggested in Acts 1:8, especially if one views Paul's goal of preaching in Rome as an important stage in the world proclamation of the gospel. Acts is thus more than history. It is a history written with a purpose of elucidating how the preaching of the gospel brings about the transformation of people through the power of the Holy Spirit.

The book begins with the experience of Pentecost. Following the resurrection and the bodily departure of Jesus, the disciples in a spirit of unity obediently gave themselves to prayer and the election of a replacement for Judas. The next event which occurred can hardly be described otherwise than as a miracle of God. Pentecost has been called by some the birth of the church. While others argue with this designation, it seems clear that the event certainly marks a very significant evangelistic moment in salvation history.

Pentecost is the point which implies the beginning of a reversal of the Tower of Babel (Gen. 11:1–9). While arguments have waged as to whether the tower builders were primarily ignorant ancient architects or cocky, plotting astrologers, it seems fair to assert that at Babel communication among people was destroyed as mankind attempted an ascent to God in an effort to show that God was little more than man. At Jerusalem, however, when the disciples began to recognize the ultimate authority of God in Christ upon their lives, the miracle of communication was restored, and the evangelistic result was astounding (Acts 2:41). From this experience a new fellowship developed. Coincident with this new spirit of fellowship came an interest in the teaching of the apostles, the common or cooperative breaking of bread (with its implications for both nourishment and worship), a commitment to prayer, and miraculous acts performed by the apostles (2:42–45). This spirit of oneness and power evident among the Christians likewise became an evangelistic confrontation with outsiders, and consequently the Lord added believers daily to the community of Christ's followers.

From Pentecost forward the Book of Acts seems to be uniquely written in such a way that almost every incident has implications for the person interested in evangelism. The healing of the lame man at the temple gate (3:1–9) is intimately linked to the message that God raised Jesus from the dead. The evangelist should not fail to note that the power operative in healing crooked limbs is likewise available to those who repent and turn from their sins (3:11–26). This miraculous story seems clearly reminiscent of the time when Jesus healed the paralytic man and then posed the question of whether it is easier to heal a sick man or forgive sin (Mark 2:9). Certainly, only the power of God can do either. Such power, Peter affirms, was made evident to mankind in the resurrection of Jesus. On behalf of all evangelists from that time to the present, Peter announces concerning that power, "We are witnesses" (Acts 3:15).

At Lystra Paul similarly becomes the agent in healing a cripple (14:8–10). This healing was regarded by the citizens

with such awe that their only conclusion was that Paul and
Barnabas must be gods. Accordingly, they hastily prepared
to offer sacrifices to the two missionaries. Undoubtedly, the
temptation to accept such high acclaim must have crossed the
minds of Paul and Barnabas, as the temptation to compromise
with Satan confronted Jesus on the mountain (Matt. 4:8–10;
Luke 4:5–8). Rather than yielding to such a temptation, however, the two Christians rushed through the streets indicating
to the people that they were merely men. In return for this
failure to compromise with Satan, Paul was soon thereafter
stoned and dragged out of the city, when Jewish opponents
from elsewhere were able to arouse hostility against the
Christian messengers. The insights for the evangelist in this
story are several. Initial positive response is no test of acceptance. People shouted "Hosanna" to Jesus on Palm Sunday
and yelled "Crucify him" on Friday. But perhaps one of the
most crucial lessons may come by way of a question. What
would have happened to the evangelistic ministry of Paul
and Barnabas if they had taken the praise of men, pretended
to be supermen, and failed to give the credit to God?

Not only at Lystra but throughout his missionary career
Paul was faced with the reality of persecution and opposition.
The two factors contributing most to the opposition against
the early Christian evangelists seem to be related to the
struggle for power, prestige, and leadership and the struggle
for economic security. Almost everywhere Paul went he confronted opposition of the Jewish leadership which saw in
Christianity a threat to the prestige and personal authority
of the Jewish hierarchy. It became clear, therefore, that the
leaders were determined to stamp out the Christian claim
that Jesus, the Christ, had brought the new age. The Holy
Spirit's powerful manifestations of the new order merely
made the Jewish opposition more intense. Opposition to the
proclamation of the gospel also arose because of economic

pressures. When Paul cured the possessed girl in Philippi, the side-show promoters of soothsaying lost their business. The resulting antagonism was vehement (Acts 16:16–24). The hostility of Demetrius, the Ephesian silversmith, was no less intense when he discovered that the Christian preachers were affecting his business profits (19:23–29). It is probably wise for anyone who would be an evangelist for Christ today to take a clue from the life of Paul and be prepared to face opposition. *When the gospel touches either a person's power or his pocketbook, he will either become transformed or raise a storm of protest.* The alternative becomes either praise to God or persecution of his messengers.

As Paul suffered persecution for proclaiming the message of Jesus, so also did the Christians in Jerusalem. Peter's healing of the lame man in the name of Jesus together with the proclamation that this Jesus was the authentic representative of God as vindicated in the resurrection was destined to bring the disciples into direct confrontation with those Jewish leaders who were behind the capture and crucifixion of Jesus. The Jewish anger and annoyance at Peter's proclamation of Jesus' resurrection (4:1–3) matured into the arrest and arraignment of Peter and John. Because of the miraculous healing and the notoriety engendered among the common people, however, the Sanhedrin directed the release of the disciples but warned them to refrain from preaching about Jesus (4:18).

Convinced that it was more important to obey God than men (4:19-20), the apostles continued to preach. Subsequently they were seized again (5:18) but were released by an angel and, to the astonishment of the council members, continued to witness in the temple (5:25). The opposition of the Jewish leadership became more intense. Under the direction of the unconverted Saul (Hebrew) or Paul (Greek), Stephen was stoned (7:54–60). And Stephen died without malice but not without calling upon the resurrected Jesus to receive his spirit.

The importance for Luke of the resurrection in the Christian proclamation can hardly be overstated. The substitute chosen to replace Judas was to become an official witness to the resurrection of Jesus (1:22). That which irritated the Jewish leadership the most was the preaching of the resurrection (4:2) because the resurrection was viewed as God's judgment of those in opposition to Jesus. The resurrection also played an extremely significant role in evangelizing the Hellenistic world. In his address on the Areopagus (Mars Hill), the division between Paul and the Athenians came at the point of the resurrection (17:31–32). The reason for the division is that the Greeks believed that man's mind was eternal or, in effect, part of God, and thus the mind was incapable of dying. But to believe in the resurrection in the sense of being made alive from the dead means that one affirms that man's essence is mortal or created and that man is dependent upon God for life both here and in the hereafter. Both Paul and Peter, according to Luke, had no doubt that man was not God nor would he ever be, and the belief in the resurrection was absolutely essential to their theologies and proclamations.

The twentieth-century evangelist must understand the centrality of the resurrection for his preaching. It is not only the vindication of the claims of Jesus; nor is it simply the example of God's power in the world. It is a fundamental statement of who man is and of God's readiness to receive him into the eternal kingdom. Accordingly, no Christian evangelist who is worthy of the name should ever be caught enunciating the age-old heresy more recently called the "divine spark of man." Man is not divine, not even the smallest particle of him! Nor is man eternal. Eternal life is a gift to man, not a human right. The story of Adam and Eve in the garden is the Bible's enunciation of how sin separated mankind from God's provision of life in antiquity (Gen. 3:22–24). The death and victorious resurrection of Jesus is the ultimate action of God in making access to eternal life available to sinful man. So significant is the resurrection that every evangelist ought to bear constantly in mind the fact that without the resurrection there would be no church and no gospel to proclaim. To speak concerning the resurrection only on Easter is a radical distortion of the Christian message.

Because the early Christians believed in the resurrection, they had a confidence that their lives were in the hand of God. Thus, the Christians prayed for boldness to speak in the midst of persecution (Acts 4:29) and rejoiced that God could use them in times of difficulty (4:21).

Nevertheless, despite their confidence in God they were still subject to the doubts and fears which can assail any human being. Ananias of Damascus had doubts about the possibility that Saul could be converted (9:13–14). The disciples in Jerusalem were very skeptical of Saul's commitment and probably considered his action a ploy to catch them off guard and seize them (9:26). But despite their fears and doubts, Ananias and Barnabas were sufficiently confident in the transforming power of God that they were willing to take the risk and accept Saul as a brother.

Perhaps one of the most touching stories concerning the humanness of the disciples who proclaimed the marvelous message of Christ's power is found in Acts 12. In seeking to please the Jews, Herod seized James the son of Zebedee and killed him. Then he imprisoned Peter (12:1–4). In the midst of such a crisis, the church's only hope seemed to be prayer, and to prayer they gave themselves with great earnestness (12:5). God's response was a miraculous releasing of Peter. After the release, Peter headed straight for the house of Zebedee where many of the disciples were gathered in prayer. But strange as it may seem, the response of the disciples to the announcement of Rhoda, the maid, concerning Peter's release was utter disbelief (12:15). Bear in mind that the disciples had witnessed many miraculous acts of God, that previously disciples had already been released by God from prison (5:19), that their most zealous opponent, Saul, had just been converted, and that they were praying for exacly what took place. Yet the response of the disciples to Rhoda was, "You are mad."

To the contemporary church, committed to the powerful action of God in evangelism, the reality of doubt, fear, and disbelief in the midst of confidence must be clearly understood. If the proclamation of the gospel depended on the consistent strength of human resources, the evangelistic mission of the church would be a blissful failure. Clearly, God does not use his people because they are strong or perfect. Instead, he uses them in spite of their weaknesses and inspires them to confidence in the midst of their doubts.

Since, therefore, the foundation of the gospel does not lie in human strength and perfection, it was not long before the church had to wrestle with the subject of *who* ought to be evangelized. From the beginning, Peter felt impelled to call the Jews to repentance (2:38; 3:19). But for the Jewish evangelists to work freely among the Gentiles necessitated a major change of attitude. Certainly pre-Christian Jews had for some time been proselytizing Gentiles, and their orientation was to transform the Gentiles into Jews. Even then, however, they really regarded Gentiles as second-class citizens. The familiar prayer in one of the Eighteen Benedictions well summarizes the view of the Jew toward the Gentile. Frequently in the course of his devotional life the Jew would pray, "I thank thee . . . that thou hast made me not a woman nor a Gentile."

This spirit of Jewish elitism could hardly be expected not

to infect Jewish Christians. Not only did such a spirit of superiority prevail among Jews regarding the non-Jews, but such a feeling was frequently prevalent among the Hebrew-speaking Jews with respect to the Greek-speaking Jews, especially those of the diaspora.[2] Some of this rivalry, no doubt, is reflected in the discontent over the daily distribution to the Greek-speaking widows recorded in Acts 6. Such a feeling of mistreatment would carry the seeds of disunity and ultimately affect the proclamation of the word. Accordingly, the church chose seven men to become the administrators of the church funds (the term "table," *trapeza,* is a colloquialism referring to financial matters or banking, Acts 6:2). The result was that complaints were handled quickly by men of high reputation, and the twelve were not impeded in their task of preaching the word of God.

The worldwide implications of the gospel message, however, were only perceived by the Christians in stages. But the fact that they remained open so that the Holy Spirit could lead them to new dimensions of understanding is a model for all succeeding generations of evangelists. The story of Philip and the Ethiopian eunuch can probably be viewed as the first stage in the development of a universal understanding of evangelism. The Ethiopian was likely a proselyte who had come on a pilgrimage to worship in Jerusalem at the Temple (8:26–28). He was apparently accepted without much hesitation as a brother believer and was baptized by Philip (8:34–39).

The story of Cornelius, the centurion, marks a progression in the realization of the evangelistic scope of the gospel. Cornelius was not a proselyte but a God-fearer, a technical term used by the Jews to indicate a Gentile who loved the Jewish God but was unwilling to pass through the necessary lustrations (washings), circumcision, and offering of a sacrifice in order to become a recognized proselyte. Cornelius remained a Gentile even though he was regarded by the Jews as a friend. But to suggest that he was part of the community of the covenant and could receive the intimate blessings of God would be far from the conclusion of the loyal Jew. The episode, therefore, involving Peter's dream of the unclean animals in which he was commanded to kill and eat that which he had never done before (10:9–16) was undoubtedly such a traumatic nightmare as to leave him feeling he was abandoning his entire heritage, especially since it happened three times and therefore should probably be received as a message from God.

No less soul-shaking for Peter must have been the experience of witnessing the coming of the Holy Spirit upon Cornelius and the God-fearers following Peter's enunciation of the incidents leading to the resurrection of Jesus and the necessity of receiving forgiveness (10:34–44). Although they were not really Jews, the only conclusion Peter could reach was that if God had allowed his transforming Spirit to come upon these people, who could deny them membership in the community of Christ? Such a conclusion was not received by the Jerusalem Christians without criticism (11:1–3), but when they heard the circumstances surrounding the expansion of the gospel to these associate-type Jews, they were unwilling to stand against the obvious leading of God. How often in the history of the church since that time has God directed his people into new spheres of evangelism by moving someone outside the immediate horizon of the community to believe in Christ? The response of the church to a new area of mission has not always been accepted willingly. But thanks be to God that many of his people are sensitive to the direction of the Spirit.

The sensitivity of God's people was also evident at Antioch as the company of Christians in that place came to recognize their responsibility for the evangelization of an-

other segment of God's world (13:1–3). Paul and Barnabas
were commissioned by the church to a new phase of proclamation that carried the Gospel to the Greco-Roman world
and to the vast multitudes of the Gentiles. Using a style in
which they began by preaching to the Jews and the God-
fearers, then the unrelated Gentiles, the gospel came by
Paul and Barnabas to Cyprus and Asia Minor. After witnessing the transformation of Gentiles in various countries,
including even the Roman proconsul [3] of Cyprus (13:12),
the two evangelists returned to Jerusalem for an historic
meeting of Christian leaders. At this council James, the half-
brother of Jesus, on behalf of the gathered assembly declared
that it was unnecessary for the Gentiles to observe Jewish
rites like circumcision in order to become Christians (15:19–
28). The responsibility of the Gentiles was limited to purity
of life-style, noncompromising attitudes in worship, and a
reverence for life as witnessed in their relationship to blood
(15:20–21, 29). Removing the bar of circumcision liberated
Christian theology from its Jewish strictures and permitted
it to become as universal as its broadening evangelistic dynamic. The entire inhabited world thus became the evangelistic goal of the church (1:8), and Christian theology became
cosmic and interracial in scope.

The worldwide goal of evangelism, however, is not simply
conceived in terms of intellectual belief. The goal is the
transformation of the whole person, and that is the reason
the church, like the early disciples, must be interested in
healing people. Moreover, the early Christians were concerned that their brethren were cared for in terms of their
physical needs. This concern reached not only the immediate
community but those in distant lands as well (11:27). In the
apostolic church, Barnabas became the epitome of the caring
person as he transferred his earthly wealth to the apostles
in order to provide for the needs of others (4:32–37). Ananias

and Sapphira, however, became the symbol of those who give, not from a sense of love, but because they wish to receive the praise of men (5:1–11). Their condemnation did not arise from how much they gave to the church, but it came because they sought to use the church for their own ends. They, like Simon, the magician of Samaria, sought to purchase the power and approval of God (8:9–24). But the self-giving God came in Christ Jesus to create a genuine self-giving community, and in such a community people like Simon Magus, Ananias, and Sapphira are obviously out of place. They proclaim themselves and their own abilities. The community of Christians is called to proclaim the resurrected, self-giving Christ.

Finally, the Book of Acts provides for the Christian evangelist examples of what commitment to God in Christ and the leading of the Holy Spirit really mean. By being sensitive to God's direction, Philip was prepared to share the marvelous message of Christ with a traveling African from Ethiopia (8:26–39). Peter responded to the invitation of a Roman soldier from Caesarea to speak about Jesus (10:1–11:18). Paul heeded the vision of a man from Macedonia and with the gospel turned west from Troas, instead of going east (16:9–10). Thus, Christianity came to Europe where it took a vital foothold. The flexibility of the disciples and their openness to God's possibilities in the world for change and transformation is a model for all who would serve their Lord as proclaimers of his message.

Yet with all their openness they were not spineless. Stephen faced the horrible death of stoning with such an assurance in God that, for Luke, Stephen virtually reflected Christ's spirit on the cross (see the forgiveness statement of Jesus which is recorded in the Gospels only by Luke at 23:34). As the first Christian martyr, the symbol of all others to follow, Stephen closes his life with a gentle but victorious dying

prayer, "Lord, do not lay this sin against them" (Acts 7:60).
Undoubtedly, this death of Stephen must have made a lasting
impression upon Saul, the promoter of the persecution. In
later years, on the third missionary journey, the great evangelist to Gentiles himself, very much like Jesus before him,
set his face steadfastly to go to Jerusalem (see Luke's description of Jesus in Luke 9:51). Despite the fact that he was
warned of certain imprisonment (Acts 21:10–11) and although both the Ephesian elders and the Christians of Caesarea wept for him and pleaded that he turn aside (20:37–38;
21:12), Paul's commitment to the leading of God was un-
shaken. Thus he answered, "For what reason are you weeping
and breaking my heart? I am prepared not only to be bound,
but also to die at Jerusalem for the name of the Lord Jesus"
(21:13). Such a conviction of God's hand on his life brought
him with confidence before Felix (24:24), Festus (25:8–11),
Agrippa (26:2–29), and ultimately to Caesar (25:12; 27:24).
In the violent storm, when the ship was smashed near Malta,
it was not the commanding Roman officer who exuded confidence but rather the stalwart Christian prisoner (27:21–44)
by the name of Paul.

The Book of Acts is undoubtedly one of the world's most
exciting literary records. It is an intriguing dramatic story
concerning the evangelistic vitality of an initially small but
genuinely transformed and determined group of human
beings who dared to face death rather than reject the evangelistic imperatives from God. Their preaching about the
power of God and their own life-commitments were insepa-
rably interwoven. Their messages and their lives bore one
focus. These living witnesses exemplified the meaning of
authentic proclamation both to others of their era as well as
to Christian evangelists of today.

But not all early evangelists were as committed as Peter,
Barnabas, and Stephen. Some struggled with gripping inse-

curity, inconsistency, and lack of understanding. For them, faithful, zealous followers like Paul accepted the crucial responsibility of setting in written form the essential advice necessary for the strengthening of Christian life and witness throughout the world. These letters are another important dimension of the biblical account concerning evangelism.

NOTES

1. F. C. Baur, *Paul, the Apostle of Jesus Christ* . . . , trans. A. Menzies (London: Williams & Norgate, 1875), 2 vols. For an excellent analysis of the Tübingen school and the significance of the theories today, see Johannes Munck, *Paul and the Salvation of Mankind,* trans. Frank Clarke (Richmond: John Knox Press, 1959).

2. The term *diaspora* refers to the settlement of Jews outside Palestine.

3. A proconsul, like Sergius Paulus, was the governor of a peaceful Roman province and was appointed by the Senate for approximately one year. During this time he was expected through the process of taxation to provide for his retirement. The province in which Israel was located was not considered peaceful and was, therefore, ruled over by a soldier-governor— legate (for a large area) or procurator (for a small hostile area)— who was directly responsible to the emperor.

5
Advice
for Struggling Evangelists

If you were on trial
for being a Christian
—would there be
enough evidence
to convict
you?

ADVICE FOR STRUGGLING EVANGELISTS

The epistles or letters form a major section of the New Testament and provide strategic advice for believers concerning the nature and style of evangelism. While space prohibits the exposition of all the epistles, the four letters reviewed in this chapter from the writings of Paul should provide an introduction to the indispensable counsel concerning evangelism which the apostolic correspondents have to offer twentieth-century proclaimers of the gospel of Jesus Christ. This advice, written centuries ago for application in an ancient society, is as relevant when translated for modern society as if it appeared in the most recent evangelistic quarterly of the church.

Encountering the Extraordinary Evangelist [1]

Paul, the apostle to the Gentiles, ranks as one of the most dynamic evangelistic figures in the history of Christendom. In reflecting on the life of this son of Israel, one cannot help but admire his evangelistic zeal that carried him across an empire in the days when sailing ships were scarcely more than modern lifeboats. Luke considered him of such importance that he filled half his treatise on the Acts with the conversion and ministry of this flaming descendant of Abraham. To study the life and teaching of this man Paul is one of the great challenges for the prospective evangelist because life and message truly intersect in this person who, after he met the risen Jesus, raised a dead man at Troas, was called a god at Lystra, was beaten and incarcerated at Philippi, created a riot in Ephesus, was dragged out of the Temple at Jerusalem, and finally died the death of a martyr.

So significant was this man Paul that he has been identified by some as the church's greatest missionary-evangelist and by others as the church's greatest thinker. If Protestantism, committed as it is to the biblical sources in contrast to tradition, was ever to choose a patron saint, it would undoubtedly have to be the passionate little Jew from Tarsus.

Of the twenty-seven books that form the New Testament Canon, thirteen are framed according to the typical Hellenistic epistolary fashion and begin with the name of a man called "Paul." These works have been variously categorized, but perhaps the designations most easily remembered are: the soteriological, salvation, or justification epistles (Gal., Rom., 1 and 2 Cor.); the Christological or Christ-centered epistles written from prison (Eph., Phil., Col., Philem.); the eschatological or end-time epistles (1 and 2 Thess.); and the pastoral or ecclesiological epistles (1 and 2 Tim., Tit.). But the above theological categorization, while being helpful, must not be interpreted in a determinative or exclusivistic fashion.

Scholarship related to Pauline studies, however, has definitely been influenced by such theological differences within the epistles. F. C. Baur, who became a key figure in the skepticism related to Acts, also has made an indelible impression upon Pauline studies. Being a Lutheran by confession, he overplayed his attachment to justification by faith alone and concluded that all the Pauline epistles except Galatians, Romans, and Corinthians were secondary and were, therefore, non-Pauline in origin. The history of Pauline studies from that point to the present has, thus, involved the authorship question. When, for instance, Albert Schweitzer concluded that Jesus was an eschatological misfit,[2] it was no longer popular to relegate interest in eschatology to the second century. Therefore, Paul was more easily associated with the Thessalonian epistles (although some regard 2 Thessalonians as a composite work). Indeed, the Epistles to Thessalonians have come to be viewed as very early epistles. Likewise, most scholars have been willing to accept the Christological writings, with some question still being raised over Ephesians. The pastorals have not yet fared as well, despite the fact that many of the individual arguments against Pauline authorship do not seem so firm as they once did. There still seems to be a predisposition to regard the combination of the arguments as being sufficiently strong to relegate the pastorals to a deutero-Pauline status, while at the same time recognizing some genuine Pauline reminiscences.

Although I recognize the authorship arguments, my purpose here is not to enter into the authorship dialogue. Rather I mention it to point out that predispositions have much to say about conclusions. Moreover, conclusions today are at least sufficiently favorable to Paul so that whatever position one takes the epistles may be treated in some sense as being related at least to Paul and certainly not distortions of Paul.

Choosing the Evangelistic Model

The person concerned with gaining Paul's perspective on evangelism could probably take his starting point with any of the epistles. Nevertheless, in the course of studying these epistles, visiting most of the ancient sites connected with Paul, and teaching Pauline studies to seminarians for over a decade, I consider that one significant point from which to begin a statement of Paul's view on evangelism is with the insights available in the Book of Philippians. Sometimes overlooked has been Paul's own personal, mature reflections concerning the nature of witnessing which he provides for these Christians who were the first recipients of his evangelistic outreach in Europe and who continued to provide exemplary support for his work (Phil. 2:25).

Philippians is Paul's enunciation of the Christian model. The citizens of Philippi were proud of the fact that their city was specially designated as a colony (with all the tax rights and privileges) in honor of the battle which decided the nature of the Roman republic.[3] To these citizens Paul enunciates a different orientation. The Christian in Philippians is exhorted not to exhibit personal or material pride but to copy the style of Jesus. Thus, he is not merely to look to his own interests but equally, if not more, to the concerns of others (Phil. 2:4). Moreover, like Jesus who emptied himself and became a servant (2:7), Paul, in writing from prison, suggests that his own life is to be viewed as a model. Accordingly, he challenges the Christians to copy or imitate him. In addition, he recommends that they recognize and pattern themselves after those in the church who are likewise such examples (3:17).

From the perspective of human nature, the orientation in the Christian model is not only frequently difficult to accept but at times almost seems impossible to believe. In the first place, the gospel and its advance is viewed as absolutely primary, and Paul virtually regards his own life situation, in effect, as unimportant. Today's skeptic, perhaps, can understand the sacrificing, nonempire-building view of a man like Paul if he thinks that Paul is rationalizing his life pattern—to the end that the imprisonment seems to be working for the extension of the gospel as other Christians are made confident by Paul's greater confidence in the power of Christ (1:12–14). But the real test for even the Christian evangelist comes in his dialogue with Paul concerning the view he takes of other Christian evangelists who seem to be selfish and envious and create tensions with Christian brothers through their style of proclamation. Paul's response to this difficult situation is that he is delighted that Christ is being proclaimed. As far as he is concerned, he will rejoice whether such proclamation is done falsely as a game or from actual conviction.

Into the competitive church situation of the Western world today where name calling among Christian brothers is sometimes observed, Paul's words seem to come with knifelike sharpness and cut to the heart of much of our self-righteous, self-oriented church-empire building. One wonders what Paul might say to Christian proclaimers of this era if he was alive. Do we proclaim Christ for our own ends or from a nonself-centered way of life?

The second aspect of the model proclaimer is probably equally as hard to accept as the first for some Christians of the twentieth century. Paul is not oriented to things like cars, bank accounts, and houses. In fact, he possesses what one might call a death perspective. When he says that for him "to live is Christ" while "to die is gain" (1:21), he means exactly what he says. The core values of his life were so radically altered on the Damascus road that the zealous persecutor of the church forever thereafter regarded himself as a slave who was subject to Christ (1:1; see also Rom. 1:1). His desire to be with Christ was the great expectation of his life. He was ready to die (Phil 1:23) and experience the resurrection (3:8–11). But unlike the Greek thinkers there was no chance that he would seek release from this world through suicide because obedience to Christ and the worldwide proclamation of the gospel were also of paramount significance to him (1:24). Thus, while he longed to die and be with Christ, Paul was prepared to live for the purpose of preaching the good news.

With respect to the nature of living the Christian life, Paul was a realist. He recognized that the Christian would undoubtedly have opponents (1:28) because Paul always took seriously the opposition of Satan. Thus, he views the Christian life in the world as having two privileges: the privilege of believing and the privilege of suffering for Christ's sake (1:29; 3:10). It was this perspective of the joyful acceptance of death and suffering that made such an impact upon the materialistically oriented Greco-Roman world. Marcus Aurelius, one of Rome's most perceptive emperors, recognized that this orientation of the Christians would virtually shake the footings of the Roman Empire, and he committed himself to the persecution of the Christians, convinced that the Christians would not carry their commitment to death.[4] He was absolutely wrong! Years after the early persecutions, Tertullian wrote that the blood of the martyrs had become the seed of the church.[5] The contemporary Christian who would pass beyond the mere name to the reality and become one of Christ's witnesses to this generation must realize that the world can sense whether the commitment is ultimate or whether the Christian still places his trust in "the flesh" and in the things of the material order (3:3–10).

The third aspect of the Christian orientation, present in the model proclaimer, is an absolute confidence in God's role within history. Running throughout the Book of Philippians is a strong trust in the *parousia* or return of Christ (see 1:6; 2:16; 3:20; 4:5). Concurrent with this eschatological expectation that the end of history is in God's hand goes a faith in the present transforming power of Christ. Paul believed firmly in God's power to transform human lives. He preached and prayed accordingly (1:3–6). He also believed that some day everyone would have to recognize the reality of Jesus as the Son of God, whether or not they were Christians who would enjoy eternal life. Although the world might seem to be in the hands of evil forces (2:15), Christians do not live in vain. They can rejoice in the midst of a perverse society (1:4, 19, 25; 2:17; 4:4) because they know the end from the beginning. They also know that the powerful God whose will must ultimately be done in history has resources to supply the needs of his people (4:19). But whether in famine or plenty, the point is not the presence or absence of material things but one's contented relationship with God (4:11–13).

Such a perspective is far from typical within the world. But it is such a confidence in God, his power for human life, and his ultimate triumph in history that enables weak human beings such as Paul to become exceedingly effective proclaimers of God's message of forgiveness and of new life in Christ Jesus. Without such confidence in God's power and activity the proclaimer is merely a babbling moralist. But to believe that God has the world's timepiece in his hand means that even in the midst of adversity, war, and persecution the Christian has a wonderful message of hope for mankind.

Clarifying the Evangelistic Message

In Paul, God chose a man with an exceedingly unique background to provide the church with a magnificent theological formulation of the significance of the coming of Christ and the meaning of the good news. The Book of Romans is a masterpiece which reflects Paul's uniqueness. He was educated in the best of the Jewish schools "at the feet" of Gamaliel. Gamaliel in turn was the student of Hillel, and Hillel is regarded by many as the foremost of the Jewish rabbis. But Paul was not only familiar with the way of the synagogue. He was born among the dispersed Jews outside of Palestine in the educational center of Tarsus, which perhaps we could liken to a Princeton, Harvard, or Oxford of today.

While some scholars like Davies, van Unnik, and Jeremias in recent days have swung to the opposite extreme from Reitzenstein and Bultmann and seem to attribute very little to Paul's Hellenistic background, such an alternative seems to be just as unnecessary as Bultmann's lack of attention to Paul's Hebraic background.[6] In his youth, Paul seems to have been a fanatical Jew who was vitally concerned with learning and preserving the best of Judaism. Similarly, there seems little doubt that Bultmann is correct in pointing out that the Tarsian was very familiar with the Cynic and Stoic diatribe, the method of current philosophic discussion in the Hellenistic world. His use of the method is clearly more than he would have gained from contact with Greek-speaking Jews in Palestine. Whether he gained his understanding of Hellenistic thought in early childhood or as a zealous evangelist to the Gentiles has been debated. Probably the best answer lies in some combination of both childhood awareness and adult Christian passion which leads the evangelist to a desire for comprehending the philosophy of those to whom he is preaching. In Paul, God chose a man of crosscultural dimensions, and even his Hebrew and Greek names Saul and Paul bear testimony to his relationship with both cultures. To this man Paul, Christianity has turned often for the structure of its evangelistic message concerning Jesus Christ.

Instead of a one-sided approach to understanding Paul, it is essential to recognize that he is thought oriented to both the Jews and the Greeks. It is likewise important to note that Paul is more than the sum of his backgrounds because the Damascus road experience transformed him into an entirely new person. Such a new synthesis can be clearly perceived in Romans. In Romans 3:22–23 (which have become favorite evangelistic verses) Paul makes the climactic assertion that in the sight of God there is absolutely no distinction between men because "all have sinned and fall

short of the glory of God." In reaching this significant conclusion, Paul has developed his argument within chapters
1 through 3 in two quite different directions. Accordingly,
he has given his readers an example of witnessing to two
very different groups of people.

In Romans 1:18 and the verses following Paul evaluates
the self-made Greeks and Romans in terms of their own
thought patterns. His method is exceedingly interesting because he employs their philosophical presuppositions to indicate the hopeless state of their lives. The wrath of God, he
states, descends upon the Greeks and Romans, not unfairly,
but because they suppress the truth as they know it and worship the created order rather than the Creator of the world
order (1:18, 25).

The argument in this chapter may seem strange to people
of the twentieth century, but the problems of the ancients
were not really very different from those of today, and their
gods were actually encapsulations of their interests. Mars or
Ares symbolized power through might; Venus or Aphrodite
epitomized pleasure through sexual indulgence; and Dio-
nysus portrayed carefree abandonment and emotional release
through alcoholic inspiration. When, therefore, Paul affirmed
that man was suppressing the truth, the Hellenistic reader
could hardly miss his point because he used a concept concerning the divisions of man's nature with which the reader
would be familiar.

Man, according to this pattern of reasoning, was said to
have been created in three parts. Starting from the bottom
of man, the genitals and the stomach represent his passions;
next the heart represents his life affirmation in the world;
and finally the mind which is highest and nearest the gods
represents his divine reason. The Greek or Roman would
admit that man's passions were low and base, but he clearly
would argue that man's mind was divinely oriented and

that the mind and the passions were distinctly separated. In showing the Hellenistic reader, however, his need for God's forgiveness, Paul begins in the center of life with the heart (1:24) and indicates that God permits the estranged heart or the selfish will to reap its own reward in the passions and actions of the body. As a result (1:26) the low passions become dominant.

When man yields to his passions, he becomes spineless. As might be expected, the mind then loses its power of acute perception (1:28) and adjusts itself to the distorted will of man. Paul, thus, clearly isolates the problem, even for the twentieth century. Because man is a unified human being, man should make no mistake about the fact that the mind can be an instrument of self-deception. Man's mind is not the measure of all things, and therefore man is in need of resources beyond his own capacity.

Paul turns next to the Jew who easily might pass judgment on the indulgent Gentile (2:1). No doubt it was easy for the Jew to think that because he had the law and the covenant that God was partial to him (2:17). Yet the words of Paul concerning such blessings need to be reconsidered. "Do you not know," avers the apostle, "that God's kindness is meant to lead you to repentance?" (2:4, RSV). The thought pattern is quite different from that employed in speaking to the Gentile. Paul is conversing with the Jew as a Jew. He argues that the wrath of God falls justly and without discrimination upon all who deserve it, both Jew and Greek (2:6–11). Those who sin not possessing the law die apart from the law, but those who sin and are under the law are judged according to the law (2:12). Disturbed by such impartiality, the Jew would probably then ask Paul concerning his view of the value of Judaism and circumcision. In order to explain this situation to the Jew, Paul uses the Hebrew idea of the heart as a basis for understanding the true sonship of Israel.

He argues that the true Jew is a Jew "who is one inwardly, and circumcision is a matter of the heart" (2:29). Such an argument should remind the Jew that the proud or hard heart in the Old Testament was consistently viewed as being opposed to God.

The conclusion should, thus, be clear. If this is the case, what is the advantage of being a Jew? The advantage is that the Jewish people, distinct from all other ancient peoples, have come to know precisely the will and purpose of God (3:2). But it is not enough to know the will of God because it is required of every man that he must do it. The point, therefore, is that while the Jews have had a distinct advantage they are no better off than others, and even the psalmist admits that they are not righteous (3:9 ff.).

In summary, when Paul reaches his conclusion that all have sinned (3:23) and need the grace of God in Jesus Christ (3:24–31), he has used both the Greco-Roman and Jewish thought patterns to present his point. He has, thus, given an example to future evangelists of how the message of Christ can be applied to different types of people with quite different orientations.

From chapter 4 through chapter 6 Paul deals with the evangelistic message of transformation in terms of the nature of justification and its implications for new life. In chapter 4 he makes it clear, in case there is any misunderstanding, that Abraham, the patriarch of the Jewish people, was reckoned acceptable to God, not by his works, but because he believed God and trusted in his promises. In chapter 5 Paul challenges his Christian reader to live the justified life in peace with God and to realize the profound implications of being both reconciled and received through God's gracious love at a time when he, like everyone, was actually a hostile enemy to God and lived according to the rebellious style of man's progenitor, Adam. Thus, in chapter 6 Paul tells the Christian to put away sin and conduct his life according to the pattern of baptism in which he died to the slavery of the old life and rose for a new obedience to Christ.

In chapters 7 and 8, a frequently misunderstood section of Romans, Paul sets forth—through a genuinely remarkable psychological analysis which is relevant even against the background of today's advanced psychological studies—a realistic picture of the nature of frustration encountered in living the Christian life and the powerful nature of forgiveness.

The answer to the Christian's frustration and lack of perfection, according to chapter 7, is not to be found in man's own resources. But the evangelistic message of recognizing human weakness and turning to God in utter dependence applies, *not simply to the initial stage of salvation, but throughout all of life.*

Hudson Taylor, the great missionary to China of the last era, discovered as many others have, the secret of real surrender when in 1870—after he had been a missionary for some time—he began to rest in Jesus from the worries and cares of life.[7] When one starts to regard his frailties from the perspective of the Savior and recognizes the nature of God's total concern for life, as Paul states in Romans 8, one begins to learn the deep meaning of real acceptance by Christ and the purpose and nature of the noncondemning God. Paul, the former Jewish zealot, after the Damascus road experience, began to reveal in his life a new type of zeal and servitude based on thanksgiving. The set of his mind focused on Christ, and he learned the style of a life patterned according to the Spirit (*kata pneuma*). Chapter 8 is Paul's enunciation of what it means for a person to live for Christ. Without this total life perspective, the evangelistic message is incomplete, and the gospel proclamation is truncated.

God's interest in man is not simply with the beginning of new life. The set of the mind and the style of the whole of life is the concern of God. Accordingly, since the almighty God does not condemn the Christian—even though he is mortal—when his life is patterned according to the Spirit and his expectation is to share in the glorification of the hereafter, Paul asks the reader what possible power is there in all of creation that could condemn the Christian or rob him of his heritage. Nothing, indeed, can separate from the victorious love of God in Christ Jesus that believer who has learned this pattern of life (8:39). Such is the basic message of the gospel, the good news to be proclaimed by Christians everywhere.

Romans 9–11 concerns Paul's prayerful consideration of his own people and their rejection because of disobedience. Paul reflects first that not all Jews belong to the promise (9:6–8, 27) and second that not all are lost (9:27; 11:25–26). Indeed, those who have and do pursue righteousness in faith through Christ shall be saved (9:30–32; 10:3–4). And since there is ultimately no distinction between Jew and Greek, the gospel is appropriate for both. All are brought to new life through confessing with the mouth that Jesus is Lord and believing in the heart that God raised Jesus from the dead (10:9–13).

In Romans 13:1–7 the role of the Christian as a citizen is briefly introduced. While Paul did not deal with all aspects of the relationship to the state, this subject is of such vital significance for the evangelist that it bears some discussion here. The Christian should clearly understand the priorities of his allegiance. Naturally, he is expected to be a good citizen and to "render to Caesar" or the state the things that belong to the state (Rom. 13:7; Matt. 22:15–22; Mark 12:13–17; Luke 20:20–26).

But the Christian must be careful in his relationship with

his country to render *first* "to God" what belongs to God (Matt. 22:22; Mark 12:17; Luke 20:25). Certainly, the payment of taxes is part of the state's right (Rom. 13:6), and if anyone refuses to recognize the state's right and authority in these matters, he must realize that there may be the possibility of punishment (13:3). Where in matters of conscience, however, the authority of the state and the authority of God collide, the Christian is duty bound to obey God even if the state has power to punish him for so doing. The Christian's first priority is to God and to the service of God. He is only thereafter a citizen of the country in which he lives. When the state demands from the Christian his religious allegiance, the state has usurped the authority of God and thereby is acting as though it is divine.

Particularly with respect to evangelism, it is imperative to understand in the days ahead that Christians may find an increasing hostility to the proclamation of the gospel. Whether because of growing nationalism and national religions, because of a number of unfortunate identifications of Christianity with some forms of Western culture, or because of materialistic, anti-Christian orientations, Christians may be given ultimatums to cease proclaiming the gospel which judges all mankind. The contemporary Christian must pray that his or her life-answer to such ultimatums will not be different from that of Peter and John who obeyed God rather than men (Acts 4:18-20). In return for such an answer the Christian may face imprisonment or death, as a number of Christians are doing today in many different parts of the world. But the loving prayer of the Christian in the face of such persecution must be for strength from God to be able to make known to non-Christians the messages of life in Christ while there is still time (Acts 4:29).

The closing chapters of Romans involve particular aspects of the Christian life as the message of Christ's salvation is applied in the world. The Christian is expected to use his God-given gifts for the extension of the kingdom (Rom. 12). He is one who, living in the expectation of the return of Christ, is to avoid all forms of inappropriate licentious and drunken conduct (Rom. 13). Moreover, he is to support those who may be weak in the faith. Thus, he is to avoid becoming a stumbling block to others for the sake of Christ's work (Rom. 14–15). Since the gospel becomes alive in God's children, Paul calls Christians to present their bodies a living sacrifice to God and to be distinguished from the world by the transforming power of God within them (12:1–2). Such is the evangelistic message of Paul, and such is its meaning for the Christian life.

In conclusion, chapter 15 provides a brief note of information which sets this entire epistle in the context of Paul's evangelistic strategy. Romans seems to be written for the purpose of strengthening the church at Rome (see 1:11–15) and of providing Paul with a firm base of Christian support from which he could launch a new evangelistic effort into Spain (15:24). In turning to the new, however, he did not forget the established churches, such as at Jerusalem, which were also in need (15:25). For Paul, a strong church, firm in its faith, was an important ingredient in developing a strong evangelistic thrust in the world. The comprehensiveness of this epistle is a striking testimony of theological acuteness which Paul expected to see in the church at Rome. Our prayer ought to be that many contemporary churches would appropriate more fully the message of Romans.

Developing an Authentic Evangelistic Community

To the Christians of Corinth—the city that honored Aphrodite, the goddess of love, with a community of a thousand prostitute priestesses and with a magnificent temple perched on the Acro-Corinthus (a lofty mountain plateau rising eighteen hundred feet above the city)—Paul addressed several letters, two of which are preserved in the New Testament Canon. As a unique contrast to the permissive, erotic city of Corinth, 1 Corinthians—with its concern for loving relationships of Christians and set in the context of a beautiful hymn on love (chap. 13)—provides the student of evangelism with what is perhaps Paul's choice statement on the nature of the evangelistic community. In this epistle Paul envelops within concrete church situations the words of Jesus concerning love being the commandment of the New Covenant and the sign of the New Community (John 13:34-35). Undoubtedly, Paul perceived that if the Christian gospel was going to make an impact upon the world Christ's disciples personally would have to represent that gospel. Basically there are probably three reactions possible to a new message. A person can accept, reject, or ignore it. The latter reaction implies that the message is regarded as mere words and irrelevant to one's life. But both Jesus and Paul knew that when the love of God is embodied in people the gospel will not be ignored.

The church at Corinth was not perfect. Such a statement hardly seems profound because the same conclusion is obvious to anyone who reads the first epistle. Yet it is precisely the fact that Paul deals herein with the imperfections of the community which makes this book so important for study. The church is not born perfect, nor does it have a perfect existence. Anyone who has been a counselor to churches and Christians knows this reality. God is not working with perfect people. He is starting with people like David, Mary Magdalene, Peter, and Thomas and molding them into a community of faith and proclamation. Paul was clearly aware of the frailty of human nature when he wrote this letter to the Christians at Corinth, but he also realized that Christ established the Christian community because Christians need one another. He also believed that the brotherhood of the church is one of the great hopes for a divided world. The purpose for Paul's writing 1 Corinthians undoubtedly relates to his desire to see the church at Corinth become a fellowship which would represent Christ's transforming love in human life and, accordingly, would challenge those outside to discover the power of God for themselves.

To this end, Paul opens 1 Corinthians with a discussion about the loveless divisions within the church, and he reminds the Christians there that their strife in terms of evangelism is counterproductive. Neither Paul, nor Apollos, nor Peter died for them. Thus, whatever name they take, if they are true to their commitment, they belong to Christ. They are brothers because Christ is not split up into sections. When they preach the gospel or baptize, it is not done in the name of Paul or Peter but in the name of Christ (1 Cor. 1:10–17). Moreover, because most Christians were not high on the economic or political ladder when they received Christ, the petty boasting among them concerning to what segment of the church they belong indicates their lack in understanding that which really counts in the kingdom of God (1:26–31). The gospel is not a message of man's strength and power. God chose what seems to man to be a foolish death on the cross to save the world (1:18). The Christian who boasts, therefore, if he boasts at all, ought *not* to boast about being a Baptist or a Lutheran or a Pentecostal follower. He ought to boast in the graciousness of God. Otherwise, he should realize that his boasting alienates his brother and that he is completely out of tune with the gospel (1:29–31).

Moreover, even in terms of witnessing, Paul reveals that man's pride can get in the way. Accordingly, the apostle is careful to indicate that in coming to the Corinthians he was

not attempting to impress them with his wisdom or elo-
quence (2:1). His concern in their evangelization was that
their faith would not rest in the brilliance of men but in the
transforming and unifying power of God (2:5). To know the
crucified Christ and to have the privilege, as a weak human
being, of proclaiming this message is Paul's greatest honor
(2:2–3).

But while expounding the brilliance of human wisdom is
certainly not Paul's purpose, he is not proposing that believers remain immature babes in their Christian faith and
life (2:6). Indeed, he is anxious for them to mature and to
learn how to evaluate the style of the world's thought and
action in terms of the mind of Christ (2:7–16). But the
problem is that as long as they argue like ordinary unre-
deemed men they will not understand the nature of world
evangelization and the husbandry of God in the entire process (3:1–9). They, like Paul, are to have a part in building
God's kingdom, but they must realize that the core of the
kingdom, the human temple, is the work of God's Spirit.
Anyone who thinks that the gospel depends on man's power
does not yet recognize the nature of the gospel (3:10–23).
Furthermore, since the gospel is a gift, those who argue with
their brothers and boast about their parties do not in fact
treat the gospel as a gift (4:7). Instead of boasting, God's
servants are called to regard all things from God's point of
view (4:1–5) and to exhibit in their lives the attitude of love
even when they are hungry, poorly clad, persecuted, and
slandered (4:9–16). The kingdom is not built by mere talk
but flows from the transforming power of God in human life
(4:20).

Because the witnessing church is called to embody the
mind of Christ, the life-style of the fellowship must be consistent with the purity and self-giving love of God. Immo-

rality is not only a sin against God, but it is also a destructive sin against the fellowship which depends upon trust and loyalty (5:9–13, 6:13–19). In a permissive society like today, one may have difficulty in accepting Paul's advice to remove an arrogant adulterer from the fellowship and "deliver the man to Satan" (5:2, 5), but Paul's prayer for the church is that God would be powerfully present in its midst and that it would not lack "in any spiritual gift" (1:7). To exclude such a man meant the preservation of the church's integrity as well as the man's possible real evangelization when he learned what it was like to live in the world apart from the restraining power against evil evident in the church through the presence of Christ (5:5).

Lawsuits within the fellowship are also regarded as destructive. Not only are lawsuits a declaration to unbelievers that the community is not a loving brotherhood, able to settle its disputes (6:5–6), but lawsuits also involve a pattern of life contrary to the style of Jesus, who suffered unfairly at the hands of his accusers (6:7). As a former lawyer, I have seen churches literally stifled when, for instance, two members of a church and of the same family hotly contested a will, or in another church when Christians have sued and countersued each other in a difficult business venture. While Paul's advice that it is better to be defrauded (6:7) sounds idealistic and lacking in realism, I could wish that some Christians I have known would have read this passage on their knees and that the church would have read it with them and supported them in this stand, even in terms of offering some financial help if necessary. When Jesus came to establish a new community through his death and resurrection (6:11), the pattern of the community was not modeled on the style of the world. Accordingly, the mere existence of an obedient community, living in the Spirit, is a proclamation to the world of God's righteous judgment on all unrighteousness and his sanctifying concern for those who love him (6:9–11).

Self-advancing use of knowledge and material rights can also be disruptive to the sense of unity within the fellowship. Knowledge has a tendency to make one proud, and therefore it needs to be tempered by self-giving, constructive love which focuses on others (8:1–3). Such, indeed, Paul says, is the case of eating food that has been offered to an idol. Since the Christian should know that an idol does not have life, the offering of food to an idol is a meaningless exercise (8:4). Clearly, the Christian is called to shun the worship of idols (10:14–22). But the Christian could, all else being satisfactory, eat the food itself without any qualms of conscience. Eating such food is in itself neither positive nor negative, and through eating or refraining from eating one does not gain points with God (8:8). But if a Christian's eating of this food would frustrate a weaker person's reasoning and conscience and lead such a one to doubt the gospel, then Paul indicates that the situation is quite different and that such eating is to be regarded as opposing the proclamation of the gospel (8:9–13).

One may, thus, experience the freedom that comes through being rightly related to God and regard all things as being lawful. Yet for the sake of his neighbor's salvation and the upbuilding of the body of Christ, the Christian will avoid many practices in life because they are not helpful in extending God's kingdom (10:23–24). As Paul testifies, although he is free from the domination of all men, he has enslaved himself to all in order that he might win more of them for Christ (9:19). Whatever rights he may have as an apostle, his goal in life is not the gaining and using of those rights but the preaching of the gospel as his gift to mankind (9:1–18). Moreover, whether in eating or drinking or preaching the gospel, he calls all Christians to copy him as he copies Christ (10:31–11:1).

The same basic perspective concerning communal unity applies to Paul's statements about women in 1 Corinthians 11:2–16. In this era of women's liberation Paul has been frequently castigated as a male chauvinist, but Paul's concern is not in the subjugation of women. Likewise one should not argue that he supported the institution of slavery merely by pointing out that he did not categorically speak out against the slave situation implied in the Book of Philemon. Actually, Paul's view concerning these matters is that the coming of Christ for the Christian should have brought an end to discrimination based on such distinctions, not only between Jew and Greek, but also between slave and freeman and between male and female (Gal. 3:28). The outworking of this theological position in society has been rather slow, but if one considers the long-range implications of Paul's advice to Philemon to receive Onesimus as a brother (Philem. 16–17), the end of slavery was definitely in sight for Christians.

In a similar fashion one should not regard Paul's advice to women as degrading, but in the society to which he was speaking his desire was to raise the status of women in the minds of men from being merely things or useful helpers to partners. In Ephesians, the long-range implications of husbands loving their wives with the same degree of commitment that Christ loved the church and died for it (Eph. 5:25–31) meant a revolution in the style of family life for the Hellenistic world. Paul's concern is that women, like men, should not be contentious and arrogant (1 Cor. 11:16) because these qualities would destroy the community's witness to society. Submission, as far back as the Garden of Eden, has been a difficult idea for human beings to understand and accept. For Paul, it was a way of life, and his slavery to Christ was far more demanding than any submission to other people.

Worship practices can also be ordered in such a way so as to fracture the fellowship. Accordingly, the Lord's Supper, which was meant to symbolize for the Christian church the sense of oneness in the body of Christ, had become a time of luxurious feasting and drinking for the more wealthy and privileged, while the poorer members were humiliated by their lack of food and drink (11:20–22). How could such activity be a winsome testimony to Christ? Instead, because of lack of discernment, it had become a profanation of the body and blood of the Lord (11:27–30). Accordingly, condemnation with the unsaved world was a possibility (11:32). But since the communion itself is meant to be a proclamation of "the Lord's death until he comes" (11:26), it is essential that at the communion service, as elsewhere, brothers in Christ evidence their brotherhood (11:33).

Even the spiritual gifts of the membership can cause problems within the church. It is, therefore, important for all Christians to recognize the diversity of gifts within the membership since not all people are made alike (12:14–26). It is, moreover, imperative that all members recognize that they form one body through the inspiration of God's Spirit (12:3–13). Thus, Christians must take great care lest they seek to make the gifts they have been given necessary appropriations for other Christians. To do so would be to suggest that Christians must be made in the image of other Christians. Nevertheless, there does seem to be in Paul's mind some sense of ordering to the gifts (12:27–31), and he indicates that the Christian ought to understand the role of the gifts. Some gifts are more personally oriented while others are proclamation oriented (14:1–36).

Paul is convinced that the Christian's task in the world

is proclamation, and his choice for the church is equated at ten thousand to a mere five prophecy over speaking in tongues (14:19). While speaking in tongues is not to be denied (14:39), it is not to be considered, as some suggest, the measure of achieving spiritual maturity. Indeed, spiritual maturity is defined in terms of love (12:31–14:1). While love is to be the aim of the Christian, the gift of prophecy or proclamation is that gift which Paul challenges each Christian to seek (14:1). To the church with its Christ-commissioned evangelistic task to the world, this exhortation of Paul ought to speak for itself!

Finally, Paul turns to the subject of the resurrection. As indicated earlier, Luke reports in Acts that the proclamation of the resurrection of Jesus Christ became a piercing reminder to the Jewish opposition that they had rejected Jesus. To the Greeks it was a challenge to their philosophical idea concerning the immortality and divinity of man. For Paul, the resurrection is the foundation for the church's preaching and the believer's faith. To deny the resurrection makes both preaching and faith meaningless (15:14). Belief in the resurrection enabled Paul to suffer for Christ, even to the point of fighting with beasts in Ephesus (15:32). Because of the resurrection, death—man's final enemy—loses its sting, and the Christian is confident that the victory will surely come through Christ Jesus (15:55–57). Thus, he labors, knowing that the work of extending the kingdom is not in vain (15:58).

In conclusion, Paul takes the pen from the hand of his amanuensis (scribe) and reminds Christians that love for the Lord Jesus is the essential quality of the Christian community which proclaims Christ and which expectantly prays for the coming of the Lord—*maranatha*—at the conclusion of time (16:21).

Becoming an Effective Evangelist

In 2 Timothy the reader discovers a context of urgency. One senses that the end of Paul's life is near and that his work is nearly finished (2 Tim. 4:6). Although some scholars forcefully argue against Pauline authorship of this epistle, the work certainly breathes the spirit of the great apostle. He is confident that he has given himself faithfully to the evangelistic task and that the Lord regards his work as well done (4:8). One cannot help feeling the longing in his heart as he repeatedly requests Timothy to come to him quickly (4:9, 21) and as he reminisces concerning Timothy's tears (1:4). The overall picture one receives is that Paul is anxious to pass on as much advice as possible to the younger man before he dies. His last written words to his young successor concerning the church's ministry are therefore very significant.

Paul opens this epistle with a charge that the young evangelist should remember his God-given heritage (1:5), calling (1:9), and confirmation in the work of Christ's church (1:6). To be an effective proclaimer of the gospel Paul affirms that one must not give in to the spirit of fear. He must instead be guided by God's spirit, wherein he can discover the resources of God's power, self-giving love, and guidance for the sound use of his life (1:7). He must learn that the God who conquered death in Christ (1:10) is dependable and will strengthen him for witnessing even in the face of suffering (1:8). When one knows this God, there is no reason to be ashamed of the gospel because God himself is responsible for protecting his work (1:8, 12). The proclaimer's task is the faithful presentation of God's message to the world (1:13–14). Moreover, he must select successors and entrust them with the good news and with the commission that they will faithfully communicate this message to others (2:2).

In the course of evangelizing the world, it will become evident that men will not be satisfied with the gospel and will seek to alter it according to their own liking (4:3), such as the insidious denial of the resurrection (2:17–18). All manner of deviations will be found as men attempt to make themselves the center of their religion and oppose the truth, even as Jannes and Jambres contradicted Moses in earlier days (3:1–8).

The role of the evangelist should not include arguing (2:14). He should *avoid like the plague such controversies* because the results of argument are love-destroying quarrels (2:23). If he disagrees with someone, he should spell out his message with gentleness in order that, if possible, his opponent might repent and discover the wonderful truth of the gospel (2:25). The evangelist's task is not to debate but to proclaim the death and resurrection of Jesus (2:11–13). In this proclamation concerning Christ the evangelist is to avoid self-oriented concerns. The ultimate results are not in his hands but in the hand of God; yet the evangelist can be confident because the Lord himself is active in the evangelistic process. Moreover, God knows the nature of the results and those who will acknowledge him (2:19).

In the evangelistic proclamation God's servant needs a clear perception of the Word of God. Therefore, he should adequately prepare himself for interpreting the message to others and not be embarrassed because of lack of understanding (2:15). The Holy Scripture which is the textbook of witnessing is a gracious gift of God. And great care must be taken by the evangelist not to treat the Bible as a book containing revealed esoteric secrets which are for the delight of the mind and intellectual conversations. The words of Scripture are meant to be appropriated in life and are given for the building of a righteous community which evidences its life in good works (3.16–17). Accordingly, the proclaimer's

concern is not with talk but with life. His purpose is to call
people to repent from sin and find new life in Christ. To
this end may all evangelists direct their efforts, and may the
Lord be with their spirits (4:22).

The magnificent epistles of Paul, though written centuries
ago, still provide prudent, timeless counsel for evangelists
of today. The wisdom of God imparted through Paul's
apostolic witness in these epistles furnishes for the church
and for every Christian evangelist an unambiguous model
of Christ-centered living and witnessing. Furthermore, these
epistles supply vital early case studies of genuine contexts
in which the gospel was presented to various people. In
these firsthand sources, the reader has opportunity for gaining a sense of Christian encounter in the early church. In
addition, the reader has the privilege of obtaining insight
into the believers' confident hope in God—a subject even
more fully enunciated in the final book of the Bible.

Notes

1. I am using some ideas from my earlier work *The Dynamics
of Pauline Evangelism* (© Gerald L. Borchert 1969) in which I
began to work out some views contained in this chapter, especially with reference to the Epistle to the Romans.
2. *The Quest for the Historical Jesus* (New York: Macmillan,
1954) is a translation of *Von Reimarus zu Wrede* first released in
1906. For a brief discussion on this point, see A. M. Hunter,
Interpreting the New Testament 1900–1950 (Philadelphia: Westminster, 1951), pp. 51–52.
3. In 42 B.C. Brutus and Cassius (assassinators of Caesar) met in
several battles with Octavian (Augustus) and Antony. On the
plains of Philippi, victory was decided for Octavian. In honor of
the victory, the entire city was rebuilt, designated a colony, and
many veterans of the war were settled there.

4. See Oscar Cullmann, *Immortality of the Soul or Resurrection of the Dead* (London: Epworth Press, 1958), especially pp. 59–60.

5. *Apology,* 50. For a stimulating treatment of the persecutions, see Herbert Workman's classic work *Persecution in the Early Church* (1906, reprinted, New York: Abingdon, 1960).

6. For a brief review of this problem, see A. M. Hunter, *Interpreting the New Testament 1900–1950,* pp. 69–71. Most introductions to Pauline studies discuss this subject in detail.

7. See Dr. and Mrs. Howard Taylor, *Hudson Taylor's Spiritual Secret* (London: China Inland Mission, 1953), especially pp. 110–45.

6
Future Perspective

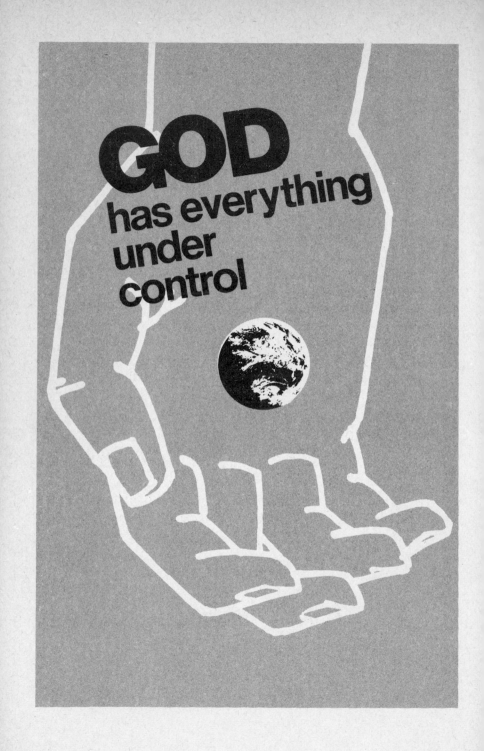

FUTURE PERSPECTIVE

As I have been writing the present study on evangelism, I have had the privilege of daily walking through the streets of Jerusalem and gazing frequently at the Temple Mount and the Mount of Olives where three religious traditions (Christian, Jewish, and Muslim) await the signal for the end of time. Moreover, I have had the exhilaration of climbing the isolated rocks of the island of Patmos [1] where the exiled John received his mind-stretching visions concerning last things. Yet these opportunities have not been an unmixed blessing because, in thinking of the return of Christ, it has also become clear that—as in the time of the early Christians—even today the idea of evangelism meets with a passionate hostility in modern Israel. [2] In these experiences a deeper sense of the evangelistic nature of the last book of the Bible has been impressed upon my mind. It is my genuine hope, therefore, that the next few pages may impart to the reader an urgent sense of the evangelistic dynamic present in this awe-inspiring "revelation of Jesus Christ" (Rev. 1:1).

At first glance most Christians hardly expect the Revelation of John to serve as a sourcebook for evangelism today. Its symbolism often seems foreign, and its imagery frequently appears strangely out of touch with contemporary reality. Moreover, the preoccupation of many interpreters with arguments concerning their schemes for the end has often frustrated adequate recognition of this book as an exciting evangelistic document. But given the strangeness of the descriptions and in spite of the tedious arguments of biblical interpreters, the reality of the end of time—the subject of this apocalypse (Revelation)—continues to thrust an evangelistic question into the hearts of most readers. Even poor biblical interpretative methods of the Revelation do not usually destroy the stark meaning of the end. The contemporary evangelist, therefore, can hardly afford to turn away from investigating this book because he is somewhat at sea in what might appear to be a verbal quagmire of symbolic pictures. Instead, the apocalypse can definitely serve as a God-given vehicle to provide a person with an important picture of man's eternal relationship with the loving and judging Lord of heaven and earth.

The Apocalypse of John ends with a great statement of purpose. This statement, however, is usually fragmented by interpreters who generally concentrate on verse 20 of the last chapter. But the affirmation of purpose begins with Revelation 22:16 where Jesus declares that he has sent his angel (messenger) to testify concerning his messiahship. The response of the Spirit and the bride to this announcement is an invitation to come. Moreover, the one who hears the reading (1:3) of this book is expected likewise to extend to others an invitation to come (22:17). The invitation is not a request for Christ to return. Instead, it is an evangelistic invitation directed to the people for whose benefit this apocalypse has been written, namely, "the thirsty" who desire "the water of life." But the warning that follows concerning tampering with the message (22:18–19) together with the proclamation of the imminent coming of the Lord Jesus (22:20) are not unrelated statements. These two subsections serve to heighten the intense necessity of considering seriously the invitation for the thirsty sinner to come and find the living water. Such is the focus of the Book of Revelation—a proclamation concerning the end and a serious call to come and discover the true source of life before it is too late!

The Book of Revelation opens with a testimonial declaration that John has witnessed a divine revelation concerning Jesus Christ and the events which are soon to follow. In the introduction, a blessing is pronounced upon all who proclaim (read aloud) this message and upon all who hear and respond appropriately. Obedient response is imperative because the eventful time (*kairos*) is near (*engus*) at hand (1:1-3). What follows this beginning is a concise statement of the gospel (*kerygma*) written from an eschatological (end-time) point of view.

The familiar Christian greeting of "grace and peace" (representing the combination of the Greek and Semitic salutations and always presented in the same order because of the priority of grace to the life of peace) is announced by none other than God—the one who makes possible and brings to fulfillment the reality of grace and peace. For those familiar with Greek, the fact that the participles referring to God appear in the Greek nominative case when the genitive is expected should not suggest that the apocalypticist (the writer) has a poor style of Greek. Rather by this simple format John is announcing to his readers that God (the provider of grace and peace) is not the object but *has been, is,* and *always will be* the subject of salvation.

Jesus is then introduced as the faithful witness (1:5), the ideal model for the Christian who is called to share in tribulation and needs strength for endurance (1:9). Because of Christ's life, death, and resurrection, praise forever belongs to him who frees us from sin by his blood and establishes us as a new community (1:5b-6). And with his coming in glory all men everywhere—even those who crucified him—will acknowledge his sovereignty in salvation (1:7).

In Revelation 1 Jesus is pictured as the wise ancient of days and stands as the symbol of stability among the golden lampstands of the churches, fully knowledgeable of all things,

incisive in his judgment, but bearing in his caring hands
the seven stars of the church. Because of this revelation,
John considers that he has seen the almighty, holy God.
Being a mere man like Isaiah, therefore, he senses that he is
undone and falls as though he is dead (cf. Isa. 6). But the
crucified-risen Christ comforts him with the words "fear
not" and reminds him that even the ultimate fears of man
concerning "Death and Hades" are subject to the Lord who
has conquered death and is alive forever (Rev. 1:17–18).
To be the messenger of such a risen victorious Savior is the
task of John, as well as the task of all who follow in his footsteps.

The letters to the seven churches in chapters 2 and 3
have been the subject of a variety of interpretations. They
have been identified with various periods of secular Roman
and medieval history as well as various periods in the history
of the church. If the Lord chooses to tarry for some time
to come, new identifications by scholars and churchmen will
undoubtedly be made and revised. The purpose of this study,
therefore, is not to add some new identifications to the long
list but to suggest for the contemporary evangelist of the
gospel that the messages to the seven churches can be
viewed as a unit.

Whatever else one may find in them, it seems clear that
these messages have something vital to say to every person
in today's church concerning his or her life-style and whole-
hearted commitment to Christ. From the overall perspective of these letters, praise or commendation is received
from the Lord for patient endurance (2:2–3, 19; 3:10), for
faithfulness in tribulation and suffering (2:9–10, 13), for
loyalty even in the face of imprisonment and martyrdom
(2:10, 13), and for constancy in bearing the name of Christ
(2:3, 13; 3:8). On the other hand, a vigorous condemnation

and a call for repentance is issued by the Lord to all those who have lost their early zeal and commitment to Christ (2:4), who have become a stumbling block to others (2:14), who follow syncretistic practices including matters of food and life-style (2:14–15, 20), who rate themselves in terms of external formalisms (3:1), and who evidence lukewarmness in matters of faith and practice (3:15). The repeated refrain throughout these letters—"He who has an ear, let him hear [obey] what the Spirit says to the churches"—indicates both the close interrelationship of the messages and the seriousness with which they are all expected to be received.

The climax in each of the seven letters is a symbolic statement concerning the hoped-for ultimate state of salvation. Attaining this state is the goal for which the evangelistic call is extended to everyone. He who hears and obeys is likened to one who will be able to eat of the tree of life (2:7) and who will receive the prized crown of life (2:10). To such an obedient one will be given the hidden manna (2:17), the new name on the white stone (2:17), and the morning star (2:28). He will be clothed with white garments, and his name will be written in the book of life (3:5). He will be established like a pillar in the temple of God and will be identified with both the name of God and God's dwelling place (3:12). Indeed, he will be given immediate access to the throne of the Lord (3:21). But it must be remembered that the fulfillment of these great promises is not automatic. Fulfillment is dependent upon the response of people to the gospel concerning Christ. Jesus is clearly pictured in the final letter as standing at the door, knocking and waiting to be welcomed by the recipients of this apocalypse. Those who hear Christ's voice and open the door will find the Lord ready to come into their lives and live with them (3:20). For the one interested in evangelism, scarcely

is there a more suitable symbolic representation of Christ—
the object of man's faith and the subject of the evangelist's
proclamation.

In turning to chapters 4 and 5, one cannot help but comment on the fact that much heat and energy have been ex-
pended by interpreters over whether or not the rapture of
the church has taken place prior to these chapters. While the
issue is certainly worthy of discussion in a commentary, for
the purposes of this study on evangelism it does not seem
to form a primary focus. It is sufficient to understand these
chapters as the stage setting for the remainder of the book.

The drama of history is unveiled in the presence of the
God of heaven and earth for whose honor the orchestral
chorus of created beings (the lion representing the wild animals; the ox representing the domesticated animals; man
representing humanity; and the eagle representing the flying creatures) sings its reverent praises concerning the eternal nature of God (4:6–8). The creatures are joined in this
exaltation by a choir of the twenty-four elders (representing
revealed religion) which glorifies God in the recognition of
his divine will in creation (4:9–11).

In spite of all the praise, however, scarcely would the
divine hand in history have been adequately understood if
it were not for the coming of God's chosen one. This special
one from the tribe of Judah was expected to be as fierce as
a lion (5:5), but upon the stage of history instead of a lion
came a lamb who appeared as though he had once been
killed. Nevertheless, although he was slain, he stands alive
in history with all the necessary power and knowledge for
mankind's salvation. Such, indeed, is the good news concerning Christ (5:6–10). The world expected from God a conquering lion. It received from God a crucified, dying lamb!
But the lamb has risen again and stands victorious.

Such a picture is symbolic both of God's vindication of

his Son's righteousness and of a guarantee to man concerning the divine offer of salvation or life from the dead. Accordingly, there follows a joint refrain of the creature chorus and the religious choir (5:9–10) which is a magnificent kerygmatic (good news) statement of the meaning of the Messiah's coming. By the blood of Christ, believing mankind throughout the world has been redeemed for God and has been made into an eschatological community of faith which looks to the day when its people will live and reign together with the Lord.

In response to this divine gift in Christ numberless voices of heaven seem to break forth into praise, much the same as the angel chorus glorified God during the Bethlehem birth of Jesus (see Luke 2:13–14). In the context of this proclamation and praise the four representatives of creation in their *amen* affirm the eternal truth of Christ (even as Paul said the world would do, see Phil. 2:9–10). Moreover, the twenty-four representatives of revealed religion can do nothing less than fall down in humble worship. The stage setting is thus complete for the dramatic unfolding of history *from God's point of view*.

While much could be said concerning the four horsemen of Revelation 6, it is sufficient for the purpose here to note that the first four seals give a rapid-fire overview of a bleak world situation. Anyone who has lived in the Middle East during some of the confrontations or some other stark experience like the European chaos of the last war, or the more recent Southeast Asian conflicts, cannot help but imagine the horrors which are here envisaged. The first rider brings the terror of an invading, conquering force. This calamity is matched by the second rider's unrestrained lawlessness which moves through the land as people murder each other. The third horseman brings economic imbalance. The food of the poor people (the wheat and the barley) skyrockets in price, while the luxuries of the rich (the oil and the wine) remain relatively the same in price. Thus, the rich become richer and the poor become poorer. And finally, the fourth horseman, portrayed in ghostly chlorine color, seems to bring the gangrenous hand of death upon the land from all sides.

At this point the fifth seal is opened, and the scene is changed to the altar of the divine drama. Here the voices of the martyrs are heard crying to God that he should avenge their blood. To all evangelists the answer which is given at this point is significant because it epitomizes one very important aspect of the message of the apocalypse. The believing martyrs are given their victory symbol of the white robe, but they are not given the privilege of dictating to God concerning the time of the end. God is in control of the world, and he knows the time of its fulfillment. He also knows all things concerning his servants. There is no question that he cares for them even though they are called upon to suffer and die for his sake. His servants are encouraged, therefore, not to worry, because—although at times it may seem otherwise—the world is ultimately in the hand of God. To die for the gospel's sake does not represent weakness and loss but strength and victory.

Yet the answer to the cry of the martyrs ultimately will come. The sixth seal is God's response in God's time. As the end appears imminent, the destruction of the cosmic realm is understood by all mankind (represented by the seven types of people mentioned in 6:15) to be God's judgment to man's rejection of the lamb. But before the destruction is completed, the interlude of chapter 7 makes it absolutely clear that God's own people are protected by God's own hand. Whether they are sealed and numbered within the appropriate number of revealed religion (144,000) or are clothed in white and numberless in the universal extent of the gospel, they are certainly reckoned within God's protection. Thus, in response to the recognition of the marvelous protective hand of God and the work of the redeeming Christ, the creature chorus and the choir of religion repeat a sevenfold benediction of praise to God. To those faithful who have gone through much suffering and tribulation for the sake of the gospel, the promise of hungering and thirsting no more and of being led by the lamb himself (7:16–17) is their great hope. This expectation is more fully enunciated in the two final chapters of this apocalypse and will be discussed again later.

As the seventh seal is opened (8:1), the reader may anticipate a catastrophic conclusion, but such has already taken place in the sixth seal. One may also expect a description of bliss, but that too has been stated in the interlude. Instead of destruction or bliss, however, one encounters complete silence—one of the most powerful dramatic experiences in the Revelation. The meaning of this silence is that the last word of God is not being told. Man will not be given the whole story, and silence reminds man of his finiteness. Both here and in the later chapter when the seven thunders remain sealed (10:4), the apocalypticist is indicating to mortal man that God reserves some aspects of knowledge pertaining to the last times for himself. Indeed, man will never know the full implications of judgment. As the martyrs could not control God's time (6:10–11), the recipients of the apocalypse are being shown a God who is ultimately beyond man's full comprehension. No man can receive the ocean of God's truth in the teacup of his mind. Moreover, no man can put God into a scheme, and no man can expect to control God's ways. Such is the God that John represents in the apocalypse. Such is the God which every evangelist must take special care to proclaim.

But at this point the silence lasts only a half-hour (8:1),

and therefore the dramatic presentation must proceed. In chapters 8 to 11 a second series of judgments (the trumpets) is detailed. Subsequently, in chapter 16 a third series of judgments (the bowls or vials) is outlined. The comprehensive effect of this threefold judgment should be obvious to the reader because it fits beautifully into the apocalyptic style. Threefold actions are undoubtedly attributed to superhuman forces. Here the judgments are unquestionably regarded as the actions of the God of heaven and earth.

In the second series of judgments the attitudes of men are discussed. The reactions here virtually recapitulate the unrepentant attitude of Pharaoh during the plagues in Egypt (Exod. 7–14). Despite the judgments, John writes, "the rest of mankind . . . did not repent" (Rev. 9:20, RSV). They continued both in wrong patterns of worship and in wrong styles of living (9:20–21). The close interrelationship here between worship and ethics is worth noting by all who are involved in evangelism because one's life-style is undoubtedly related to one's view of God. It is also of interest to note that the judgments of God are not able to bring about repentance in some people. Accordingly, the evangelist should also have a sane estimate of what he can accomplish for Christ in witnessing to the world.

The chapters which follow the second series of judgments add some important perspectives on the nature of the prophetic and evangelistic roles of God's servants. In chapter 10, the eating of the little scroll which is sweet to the mouth and bitter in the stomach (10:9–11) is reminiscent of Ezekiel's experience (Ezek. 2:8–3:3). The meaning of such symbolism seems to be that the initial reception of God's word by his servant is welcomed. The resulting implications of such a revelation for God's prophetic spokesmen, however, are often more difficult to accept. The message of God usually has two forms depending upon whether his word has been honored or has been rejected. The role of the prophet or evangelist is not only one of communicating a message of blessing but also that of proclaiming a word of doom to disobedient mankind.

Revelation 11 well illustrates another aspect of the reactions which a representative for God can expect when the task involves proclaiming God's judgment or wrath. The two witnesses of chapter 11 preach that God's judgment is coming upon the great city wherein the Lord was crucified. In the apocalypse this city is depicted as the center of the world's rejection of God. The state of the city, Jerusalem, here is symbolically likened to the role which Sodom or Egypt played in the Old Testament. The mistreatment suffered in this city by God's witnesses and the silencing of their testimony, however, brings only a brief respite to these disobedient citizens. The judgment of the Lord is certain even though it may appear to be delayed. The end comes as the seventh trumpet inevitably sounds. The world transformation takes place and Christ begins to reign forever and ever (11:15). The praise of God is recited by the twenty-four elders, and amid apocalyptic, earth-shaking phenomena the way of access to God in heaven is supernaturally opened. The second proclamation of judgment and bliss is thus completed in chapter 11.

At this point in the Apocalypse of John, there is a slight change in emphasis, and the nature of the cosmic warfare is explained in some detail. Whatever may be the particular view one espouses concerning chapters 12 through 14, the lesson for the evangelist here is that he should be clear on the nature of the opposition which he faces. He must also be aware of the ultimate result of the conflict between God and the forces of evil. Whether the woman in chapter 12 is Israel, the church, or some other symbolic figure, it seems apparent that the male child is Christ Jesus. The great red dragon is represented as being extremely powerful and in direct opposition to Christ. The dragon, however, does not possess ultimate power and is soundly defeated in the heavenly war. He, therefore, shifts his attention to the earthly realm and opposes the offspring of the woman—those "who keep the commandments of God and have the testimony of Jesus" (12:17). Proleptically, however, the apocalypticist reminds the reader that victory is definitely assured to the Christian through the blood of the Lamb. The accuser does not have power to distort a person's record with God (12:10–11).

Yet the presence of the hostile dragon in the world is clearly a problem for the Christian's life and witness (12:12b, 17). Moreover, the dragon is not without his supporting evil forces which combine as a kind of evil "trinity." They seek to control the various aspects of men's lives and attempt to gain men's allegiance. In these chapters the alignments are explicitly defined. The apocalyptic contrast between the dragon who stands on the shifting sand (12:17) and the Lamb who gathers his forces on the solid limestone rock of Mt. Zion (14:1) seems uniquely parallel to the contrast in the parable Jesus told concerning two men who built houses on the sand and the rock (see Matt. 7:24–27; Luke 6:46–49). There is, in the apocalypticist's view, no mistaking a person's commitment despite all of the fence sitting that sometimes may seem to be present among people in relationship to Christ. The servants of evil distinctly bear on their foreheads or hands (Rev. 14:9) the unholy and imperfect imprinted number 666 (or 616)[3] which is the mark of the Beast (13:18). In contrast, the names of the Lamb and of the Father are written clearly on the foreheads of the believers (14:1). The opponents are, thus, unmistakable, and the ultimate conflict is inevitable.

In setting forth the protagonists and their commitments,

the goals of the apocalypse are at the same time almost incidentally, yet quite clearly, spelled out by three angels in chapter 14. These goals are: (1) calling forth faith or the summons to fear God in relation to the proclamation of the gospel (14:6–7); (2) announcing doom upon the enemies of God (14:8); and (3) encouraging the saints to endure through an absolute commitment to the commands of God and faith in Jesus because there is a clear conviction that the present troubles of believers are nothing to compare with the ultimate troubles to be experienced by the followers of evil (14:9–12). Every Christian evangelist should be conscious of these goals of John because they relate directly to extension of the gospel.

Another unique aspect of the apocalypse is that while warnings are frequently sounded and much is said concerning preparations for the final day, the ultimate battle is hardly described in this book. The writer of the Revelation is certain of the results of the conflict. The opponents of God can do nothing else but lose. The battle is, therefore, not so much a matter of fighting as it is the climactic judgment of God. Accordingly, the angels of destruction are released at God's command, and the wine press of God's wrath is filled to capacity. The statement of blood flowing up to the height of a horse's bridle for sixteen hundred stadia (14:20) is a ghastly picture of the length of the land of Israel—the apocalypticist's reference point—bathed in blood on the Day of the Lord, a day which Amos in the Old Testament warned would be gloom and not brightness (Amos 5:18–20).

Revelation 15 brings the transition to the third and final series of judgments or plagues. It begins in magnificent form with the songs of Moses and of the Lamb which interrelate the hand of God in the Exodus with the judgments of God through Christ in the New Age. The message of the

seven bowls or vials (chap. 16), however, is much briefer
than the previous two series. In the sixth bowl the assem-
bling of the evil forces at Armageddon—the mountain of
Megiddo—is announced, but the fate of the battle is not discussed. Instead, the seventh angel merely announces, "It is
done." Thus, the apocalypticist proleptically suggests that the
outcome of opposition to God at Armageddon will be as
futile as was Pharaoh's opposition to the Israelite followers
of God at the Red Sea.

The theme of the conflict, however, is more fully discussed
in chapters 17 to 19, so as to lay to rest the issue once and for
all. The organization of these chapters from the point of view
of a proclaimer of God's message is most interesting. They
are introduced with the words of an angel, "Come, I will
show you the judgment . . ." The subsequent reaction of
John to the vision of the harlot, Babylon, is one of intense
wonder because Babylon is beautifully adorned, amazingly
wealthy, extremely powerful, and incredibly cruel in killing
the followers of Jesus. But like many people, John at this
point was not looking at the harlot with the eyes of God.
Accordingly, his vision needed clarification. Whatever may
be one's interpretation of the seven heads and the ten horns,
it is certain that in the war with the Lamb the enemies of
God are no match for the King of kings (17:7–14). Moreover, it is exceedingly interesting to notice that evil is self-
destructive because the horns and the beast consume the
beauty of the harlot and leave her naked (17:15–18). The
songs which follow are instructive. The righteous judgment
of God on evil is certain, and those who place their trust in
riches and power cannot help but bemoan the fact that in the
rape of Babylon all their values are reduced to rubble
(18:9–19).

John Bunyan magnificently caught the spirit of the apocalyptic summons of Revelation 18:4, "Come out of her, my

people, lest you take part in her sins, . . ." when he wrote
Pilgrim's Progress[4] in which he issued the call to all Christians to flee from the City of Destruction. The destruction of
this great city, according to the earlier John, does not only
bring forth regrets from the disobedient, but it also elicits
from heaven rejoicing and hallelujahs because "the marriage
of the Lamb has come, and the Bride has prepared herself"
(19:7).

With this marvelous proclamation of victory, John falls at
the feet of the angel who has been showing him these revelations, and he begins to worship the angel. But here as elsewhere in the apocalypse (22:8–9), John is quickly castigated
for this act. He is informed that even a heavenly messenger
is merely a servant of God, just like those mortals who are
devoted to the witness of Jesus. Thus, John is strictly charged
to "worship God" alone.

Finally, after all these preliminary matters are discussed,
only then is Jesus, the Word of God, introduced as the
great warrior. The ultimate battle is hardly mentioned except to indicate very briefly that the enemies of God as-
sembled and were either captured or killed by the sword
which is the tongue of the King of kings. The reader who
delights in war stories will probably find the battle scenes
here disappointing because the forces of evil seem to be
so powerless and the battle seems so lopsided. For the
evangelist, however, who has proclaimed that the war was
virtually won in the resurrection of Christ, chapters 17
through 19 merely confirm his testimony. As Oscar Cullmann[5] so vividly intimated, in the cross and resurrection
Christ won the eternal "D-day." What remains to be witnessed is God's "V-day."

In turning from chapter 19 to chapter 20 John shifts his
attention. The opening verses of chapter 20, however, contain what is probably one of the most debated parts of the

New Testament. Many Christians become extremely ada-
mant concerning their convictions and commitments in
relation to the meaning of the thousand years or the millennium in verses 2 through 7. My intention here is not to
debate the issue but to point out several facts about this
chapter which are worthy of note for evangelists. First, the
thousand years are pictured as a wonderful time when Christ
shall reign, and all who share in this first resurrection are
blessed, indeed because the ultimate power of death has no
authority over them. Equally important in this chapter for
the evangelist is the proclamation that there is an inevitable
judgment at the end of time from which there is no escape.
The judgment significantly falls upon mankind, not in terms
of what a man thinks he is or says he is, but in terms of what
he is and what he does (20:12–13).

For Christians who correctly preach about justification by
faith and affirm that no person can boast before God (Eph.
2:8–9; Rom. 3:27–28), it is equally important to remember
to preach about judgment by works because we are intended
to become God's workmanship, created for the purpose of
living exemplary, changed lives (Eph. 2:10; 2 Tim. 3:17;
James 2:14–26). Finally and very significantly, it is instructive to consider that this chapter which has been the focal
point of a number of church splits is the same chapter which
contains the great biblical proclamation of the final downfall
of the devil. Perhaps, however, Satan has been more clever
than many Christians realize. It seems as though Satan has
managed to shift the attention of the church away from his
own destruction and to concentrate the church's interpretative efforts upon a *term* like millennium which appears
only here in these few verses of Holy Scripture. In so doing,
Satan seems to have been able to raise among Christians all
sorts of disputable theories concerning these verses, perhaps

so that Christians might forget to concentrate on their wonderful hope and the certainty of Satan's downfall.

With respect to the preceding analysis, I am not suggesting that these or any other few verses of Scripture are unimportant. But I ask Christians to declare a moratorium on criticizing other Christians with whom they disagree on this subject and focus their attention on winning the lost world to the great hope of the end time. Christians must never forget that those who are not able to find this wonderful hope are scheduled, in accordance with the apocalypticist's statements, to experience an utterly horrible end. May it not be said of Christians, therefore, that they are playing little loveless games while people in the city of destruction are dying without the hope of ever experiencing the glorious promises of chapters 21 and 22.

In the concluding chapters of the Revelation, all the hopes of Christians focus in the words from the throne: "I am making all things new" (21:5). What believer will fail to feel an exuberant thrill when the eschaton will finally be realized and the announcement is made, "Behold the actual presence (skēnē) of God is with men" (21:3)? Then will come to pass the promise of God by the prophets and the apostles, "I will be his God and he shall be my son" (21:7, RSV). And then, indeed, God "will tabernacle (skēnoō) with them, and they will be his people" (21:3). To the thirsty who have known the meaning of living in desert lands, God promises, "Out of the fountain of the water of life I will give the right to drink as a free gift." Moreover, according to the Alpha and the Omega (the God of eternity), adversity will be finished (21:6). The old heaven and earth will have passed away. Gone also will be the fearful sea which terrified the ancient nonseafaring Israelites (21:1). But more important, gone forever will be weeping and pain and even death. These belong to the present mortal life but not to the life hereafter (21:4).

The new Jerusalem will be made ready as bride to be received by the Lamb. This great new city which will come down from God is symbolically pictured as a cube (21:16), one of the most perfect geometrical figures known to the ancients. The materials of its construction will be priceless (21:18–21), and to those of the Middle East who have known the reality of little rain and much drought there will be plenty of water within its walls (22:1). Unlike any experience known to man, there will be in this new Jerusalem no need for illumination because the darkness of night will no longer exist (21:22–25). There will be here no necessity for a manmade temple or place of worship because the almighty God and the Lamb will be within the city (21:22). Moreover, the tree of life from which mankind was excluded according to the first book of the Bible (Gen. 3:22–24) will be available in the time of the last chapter of the Bible. This tree which symbolizes life is a wonderful picture of the nature of heaven. It will grow on both sides of the river and thus will exemplify the fact that there is no wrong side of the river (or tracks) in this new city. Moreover, it will yield fruit every month of the year so that there is no time when man will be left hungry and without a harvest (Rev. 22:2–3). What a wonderful message of God's provision and man's expectation.

But this hope is not promised to all. The apocalypticist makes a definite effort to remind his readers that those who are cowardly, unbelieving, polluted, murderers, sexually immoral, sorcerers, idolators, and *all* liars should not expect to experience this life with God. Their expectation is clearly the horrible second death which is described as the lake which burns with fire and brimstone (21:8). In the final chapter, the apocalypticist associates these hopeless ones with the dogs who dwell outside the city gates and are not permitted to enter (22:15) even though the gates are never shut (21:25).

The message of the Revelation of John is a twofold statement. It is a proclamation of hope and an incisive word of warning. It is in fact an authoritative example for all evangelists of the twofold nature of witnessing. The proclamation of the gospel and the promises of the future involve not only joyful life but also tragic judgment. Knowing, therefore, that mankind without Christ is headed for judgment, Christians who hear this message are called to join the Spirit and the Bride in inviting all those who thirst for the water of life to come and find Christ Jesus as Lord (22:17). This Lord, indeed, is coming to receive his own. May all Christians, therefore, both join in the *maranatha* prayer for Christ's return (1 Cor. 16:22; Rev. 22:20) and find fulfillment in a genuine, loving witness to others.

NOTES

1. This barren island, which measures about ten miles long and six miles wide and lies about thirty-five miles from mainland Turkey, certainly would have served as an excellent prison island.

2. Protestant Christians should be aware of the stifling effect which the continuing results of the Medieval Muslim Millet system of closed religious community structures has had upon evangelistic efforts in the Middle East. Linked with the heritage of this social structure in Israel is an intense Jewish hostility toward the Christian proclamation. This hostility is clearly evident in organizations like the militant Jewish Defense League but also among moderate politicians who, knowing the meaning of persecution experienced by Jews in other lands, continue in their refusal to adopt a bill of rights for the state of Israel. To

give genuine freedom to others when one is in power appears to be one of the most difficult ideals for human beings to achieve.

3. Some manuscripts read 616 which probably reflects an early interpretation that Nero was more clearly designated by this number than 666.

4. Every evangelist should read this classic that was first published in 1678.

5. Oscar Cullmann, *Christ and Time,* trans. Floyd V. Filson (Philadelphia: Westminster, 1950).

7
Reaching Out

Dare to REACH OUT !

REACHING OUT

Now that you have completed this brief review of the biblical summons to evangelism, what does the outward dimension of the Bible say to you and how will our Lord's command to reach out to others affect your life?

Will you help write the conclusion to this book with a genuine attempt to become a contemporary witness for Christ? In seeking to fulfill this command to witness, you will undoubtedly experience a sense of your own human limitations as did the men of God in the Old Testament. You will probably struggle with the real significance of the coming of Jesus Christ as did the Gospel writers. You will likely yearn for the power of the Spirit in reaching out to others as was evident among the early Christians in the Book of Acts, and yet you will find that the weaknesses of their prayer life will remind you of your own frailties. You will quite possibly be moved to consider your own inconsistent evangelistic life-style in comparison to the model which Paul set for the Christian and the church. And you will indubitably wrestle with the ultimate goal of your life and the destiny to which your future is pointing as suggested in the Book of Revelation. In such a review of your life you may find that you do not measure well against the summons of God. Yet bear in mind throughout the evaluations of yourself that God chose to win the world, not by mighty revelations in terrifying acts of power, but through the incarnational pattern wherein he sent his Son to be fully human in order to show to weak humans the divine bridge of acceptance to God.

The early disciples were never less vulnerable than Christians of today. But in the midst of their humanity they discovered that the power of God was more than sufficient to overcome all the wiles of the devil. Thus, in spite of all of their infirmities and persecutions they were able to praise God for the privilege of witnessing. The results of their testimonies were staggering. In responding to God's summons they found a God was with them who was far more alive and powerful than any opposition. Bad dreams like "God is dead" did not and will not have much impact on those who have seen the power of God transform human lives. Such dreams only affect those who sit on the fence and speculate. The Christian is called to witness actively for Christ.

What, my friend, is your response to the summons of God on your life? Will you reach out to others?